A New Day For Women: Life & Writings Of Emily Spencer Kerby

Anne White, Editor

Published by Alberta Records Publication Board
Historical Society of Alberta
General Editors:
David W. Leonard and
David C. Jones
Vol. XV

Copyright © 2004 by The Historical Society of Alberta

Library and Archives Canada Cataloguing in Publication

Kerby, Emily Spencer, 1859-1938.
A new day for women : life and writings of Emily Spencer Kerby,
1859-1938 / editors, Anne White, David W. Leonard, David C. Jones.

Co-published by Alberta Records Publication Board.
Includes index.
ISBN 1-55383-029-6

1. Feminism—Canada—History—Sources. 2. Women in the
Methodist Church—Alberta—History—Sources.
I. White, Anne, 1946- II. Leonard, David, 1945-
III. Jones, David C., 1943- IV. Alberta Records Publication Board.
V. Historical Society of Alberta. VI. Title.

HQ1455.K47A25 2004   305.42'0971
C2004-905401-5

First printing 2004
Printed and bound in Canada

Published by
The Historical Society of Alberta
Alberta Records Publication Board
Box 4035, Station C
Calgary, Alberta
T2T 5M9

CONTENTS

Dedication   v
Notes on Editing and Sources   vi
Abbreviations   vii
Acknowledgments   viii
Introduction   ix

Chapter One
The Alberta Context   1
"Dainty Piece of Humanity"   1
"Don't Talk of Such Things"   3
"What Are We Coming to!"   4
"Eighteen Months for a Ruined Life"   5
"High Ideals"   5
"Church History in Calgary"   8
"Affordable Vacations for Women and Girls"   14

Chapter Two
Social History Through Stories   19
Young Love Conquers All   19
"No Telling What Might Happen"   32
"The Brown Thrush"   40
A Cautionary Tale   46
A Western Welcome   52

Chapter Three
Women and the Church   59
"A Wee Tiny Rosebud"   60
"Please Someone, Explain 'Femininity'"   65
"Good, Jolly Brothers" Versus Suffrage   66
"Paul Was a Victim of Custom"   67
"I Believe"   68

"Ye Gods! Do I Wake or Am I Dreaming"   70
"Women – The Very Best of Church Workers"   74
"Wimmin and Wine"   75

Chapter Four
Perspectives   79
"The Passing of the Servant in the Home"   79
"Plague Spot on the Race"   83
"Women's Independence for the Sake of the Race"   86
"Born a Man, Died a Senator"   89
"A Minister of Maternity"   91
"Marriage as a Career"   94
"It Was a Man Who Founded Harems"   96
"No Jury of Women"   100
A New World of Work   102
"If the Sun is to Blame, Don't Blame Us"   104
"To Produce the Finest Fruit, We Thin out the Blossoms"   110
"The New Day for Woman"   117
"Shall Married Women Work?"   121
"The Sterilization Act of Alberta, Canada"   123
Come the Revolution   125

Epilogue   131
Index   134

DEDICATION

To the memory of Emily Spencer Kerby

MY CREED

I believe in <u>Home</u> as the foundation of the Kingdom of God.
Child learns love of God in Mother's love.
Every mother is a possible Mary.
Every father a possible Joseph.
Every babe a possible Messiah.

Emily Spencer Kerby

NOTES ON EDITING AND SOURCES

Emily Spencer Kerby wrote under a variety of pseudonyms, and researching and reconstructing her writing career has proven an intriguing exercise in detective work. From the archival sources under George Kerby's fonds at the Glenbow-Alberta Archives in Calgary and Mrs. Kerby's personal fonds at the Provincial Archives of Alberta in Edmonton, I have discovered most of the pen names used in her written work. The University of Calgary Microfilm Department helped as it too holds several pieces of her writing. In addition, thanks to a University of Calgary research grant, I stayed for nearly a month in Toronto to research extensively at the United Church of Canada Archives. This research trip was invaluable as it enabled me to piece together some of the scattered material from Alberta and also to confirm several hypotheses.

This book contains both published articles and unpublished manuscripts. Where I could access a manuscript and a published article of the same work, I have provided the text from the publication.

To facilitate reading, I have introduced paragraphing, corrected spelling, added the occasional word, and introduced punctuation where necessary. Where words are illegible, omitted or added, I have indicated these with the customary brackets[ ].

Photographs documenting the life and work of Emily Spencer Kerby are sparse, but enough exist to capture important moments.

Anne White, March 21, 2004

ABBREVIATIONS
ARCHIVAL SOURCES:
GAA — Glenbow-Alberta Museum Archives (Calgary)
MRCA — Mount Royal College Archives (Calgary)
PAA — Provincial Archives of Alberta (Edmonton)
UCCA-AC — United Church of Canada Archives (Alberta Conference), PAA (Edmonton)
Ms — manuscript

WOMEN'S CLUBS AND AFFILIATIONS
NCWC — National Council of Women of Canada
WCTU — Woman's Christian Temperance Union
FWIC — Federated Women's Institutes of Canada
PCW — Alberta Provincial Council of Women
CLCW — Calgary Local Council of Women
MWMS — Methodist Women's Missionary Society
NCWC — National Council of Women of Canada
IODE — Independent Order of the Daughters of the Empire
CWC — Canadian Women's Club

ACKNOWLEDGMENTS

I have many people to thank for their support and guidance in the publication of *A New Day for Women.*

I wish to thank the Alberta Records Publication Board for providing me with this opportunity to present the work of Emily Spencer Kerby. A special word of appreciation also goes out to Drs. David Jones and David Leonard for their guidance throughout the production of this book. Further, I wish to thank Dr. Sarah Carter for her support and encouragement during my research and studies at the University of Calgary. I also want to especially acknowledge the Department of Religious Studies, University of Calgary, for the support I received during my studies. Finally, I wish to acknowledge and thank Vicki Irvine, a past Mount Royal women's studies student, who graciously gave me several photographs of the Spencer Kerby and Kerby gravesites.

To assist publication of this volume the Historical Society of Alberta gratefully received $ 5,000 from the Elise Corbet estate.

INTRODUCTION

EMILY SPENCER KERBY, 1859 -1938
LIFE AND TIMES

Emily Spencer Kerby was a prominent social activist and educator in Calgary from 1904 until her death in 1938. As a leader in the women's community, she introduced, shaped and also routinely documented many of the social campaigns of her time. During the first three decades of the twentieth century, she wrote on a wide variety of issues — many of which were controversial in so far as the topics often breached the acceptable bounds of "polite" society. Her writings addressed many of the issues important to women in an era that saw rapid changes in society, dress, conduct, and personal freedom.

Emily published at least 45 articles either under her own name or under various pseudonyms. She was a regular contributor to several magazines and periodicals, and from the existing records, it appears that most of her work was published in *Woman's Century,* the *New Outlook,* the *Christian Guardian, The Arrow, The Maple Leaf,* and the *Calgary Daily Herald.*

As part of an innovative, politically oriented and ambitious group, Emily worked within a high profile community of social activists in Alberta that included Henrietta Muir Edwards, Nellie McClung, Louise McKinney and Emily Murphy. Further, linked by many of the same causes espoused by the service clubs of Calgary, Emily worked alongside noted clubwomen such as Alice Jamieson, Maude Riley, Annie Gale, and Anne Langford. Her own contribution, however, is the subject of this book, and it was a unique and unforgettable legacy.

BEGINNINGS

Emily Spencer was born in Toronto, Ontario, on March 25, 1859 or 1860.[1] Her mother was Sarah Lafferty (1818-1892), and her father was the Rev. James Spencer (1812-1863). The Lafferty and Spencer families were Methodists and United Empire Loyalists who had migrated to British North America in 1777 during the War of Independence. Lafferty and Spencer were married in 1843, and they had nine children, six of whom would survive into adulthood.[2]

Emily was an intelligent woman who graduated from the Toronto Normal School in the mid-1880s. She later became principal of a large public school in Paris, Ontario. In 1888 she met George William Kerby (1860-1944) in Woodstock, Ontario. George was a newly ordained minister, and through the influence of his preaching, a revival had occurred in the area in 1888. After a short courtship, the couple married on October 11th of that same year. According to social custom, Emily was required to resign her position as principal of the Paris Public School shortly before her marriage.

Few details surrounding the next twelve years of Emily Kerby's life have survived. She served with her husband in Methodist pastorates in Woodstock, Hamilton, St. Catharines, Brantford and Montreal. In 1901 George Kerby was selected by the Methodist Conference in Toronto to be a travelling revivalist preacher. Together with his preaching partner, the Rev. George Turk, George Kerby travelled throughout Canada and the United States over the next two years, the two forming an effective evangelistic team. As a consequence, George saw little of his wife and their two children, Helen Jalvera and Harold Spencer.[3]

By the time George returned home from his preaching tour in 1902, his reputation as an evangelist was established. As a popular Methodist preacher, he now received many invitations to pastor at affluent, settled churches in eastern Canada. Emily, however, had other ideas, and when George received an invitation from a church on the frontier — the Central Methodist Church in Calgary,

---

[1] Existing biographical notes list the date as 1859. However, as can be seen by her tombstone, the date is 1860. Possibly, Emily's birth was adjusted to ease the social discomfort in her appearing older than her husband.

[2] Obituary, "Death of Mrs. James Spencer," *Christian Guardian*, January 20, 1892, p. 37.

[3] MCRA, John Howse, *A History of Mount Royal College*, unpublished manuscript, n.d., Chapter V. p. 4.

then in the Northwest Territories — her interest grew. Though some cautioned George that he would fade into obscurity out west, Emily rose to the challenge and suggested he accept the position.[4]

In July 1903, the Kerbys arrived in Calgary. The Calgary press gave full coverage to Reverend George, but said very little regarding Emily. From this time on, however, Emily began to emerge from her husband's shadow.

In the early years in Calgary, Emily played the stereotypical role of a pastor's wife, participating in church functions and organizations. Gradually, however, she began to emerge in her own right, exhibiting exceptional leadership, preaching and teaching abilities. In 1910 she was listed as a class leader — one of only two women, alongside six male counterparts.[5] Female class leaders could be appointed if they were either deaconesses or ministers' wives. In the latter instance, only those wives who showed competency and strong leadership capabilities were appointed. In 1912 Emily — or "Mrs. G. W. Kerby" — was listed as leader of the Anti-Knockers' Bible Class.[6] The Anti Knockers were a prestigious group of young men at Central Methodist, considered to be the promising new leaders in the church.

YOUNG WOMAN'S CHRISTIAN ASSOCIATION

By 1907 Emily had established herself as a leader in the Calgary women's community. The earliest evidence of her leadership ability can be found in the minutes of the Young Woman's Christian Association. On July 2, 1907, she convened a meeting at Central Methodist Church to discuss the accommodation crisis faced by single, immigrant girls and women on their arrival in Calgary. The meeting opened with prayer led by Mrs. Kerby, and among the

---

[4] Ibid.

[5] J. Frazer Perry, They Gathered at the River: 1875-1975 (Calgary: Northwest Printing, 1975), p. 303. A class leader was a lay person who was appointed as leader of a specific group of men or women within the Methodist congregation. The respective classes would meet in their groups for prayer and Bible study, mutual support and community guidance. The practice dated back to the eighteenth century Evangelical Revival in Britain. At that time, the newly emerging Methodist movement grew so rapidly that it was feared that individual attention to the new believers might be overlooked. The class leader's responsibility was to provide teaching and guidance within a personal and friendly environment.

[6] The title "Anti-Knockers" probably refers to the powerful opposition to critics during the settlement boom.

Opening of the YWCA, Calgary, 1911. Emily is second from left, back row. GAA, NA 2315-2.

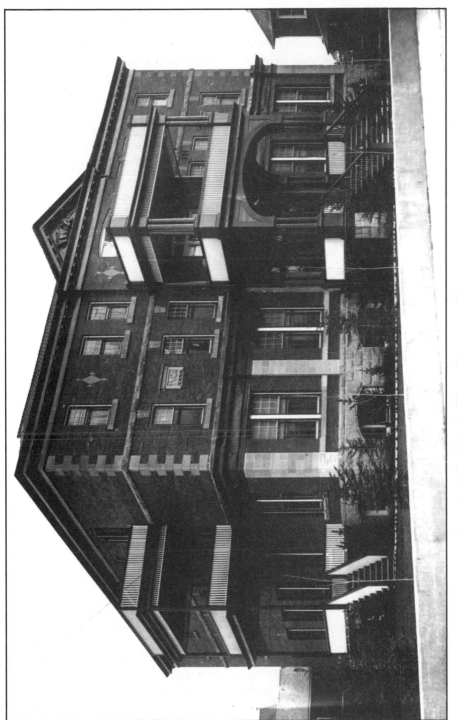

The splendid YWCA Building, Calgary, c. 1911. GAA, NC 24-13.

prominent women present were Mrs. John McDougall, Mrs. G. S. Jamieson, and Mrs. Thomas Underwood. Emily led the meeting, and each woman present agreed to raise $100 for the cause.[7] By November 4, 1907, enough money had been raised to pay one month's rent on a selected property. Mrs. Kerby moved that the accommodation be immediately rented and, that same month, the Calgary YWCA was opened.

As part of the on-going aggressive fund raising campaign, the YWCA took charge of the publication of the *Calgary Daily Herald* newspaper for one day. The owners of the *Herald* were Methodists who had agreed to donate all proceeds of newspaper sales for July 31, 1909, to the fledgling YWCA. In the publication project Emily was managing editor.[8]

By the year 1910, there was a YWCA Travellers' Aid program which assisted women and their families in their treks through the Province and into British Columbia. By 1912 the YWCA was offering social service and training programs for women, together with swimming and basketball tournaments. Also, summer camps and facilities in Banff, Lake Louise and Field provided affordable vacation accommodation for working class women.[9] Emily was elected honorary president of the YWCA in 1907 and would serve the organization in various capacities until the early 1930s.

MENTORSHIP AT MOUNT ROYAL

In 1911 George Kerby left Central Methodist Church to become principal of the newly established Mount Royal Junior College in Calgary, then designated as a Methodist co-educational, residential secondary school. Emily was appointed co-principal.[10] She also taught the junior grades for years, but officially she was never recognized in these capacities by the board of directors of Mount Royal College, and she never received even token remuneration for her services.[11]

---

[7] GAA, M.1711/2 (YWCA) Board Minutes, July 2, 1907, 1711/2 (YWCA) Board Minutes, July 2, 1907.

[8] *Ibid.*, May 21, 1909.

[9] "YWCA Committee Makes Presentation to Mrs. G. W. Kerby," *Calgary Herald*, October 13, 1923; YWCA Board Minutes, May 21, 1909.

[10] Jean Grant, "In Memoriam," PAA, UCCA-AC, Acc. No. 75.387, Box 181, Item 6031. Grant states that the Kerbys "set about the organization necessary, and later were prevailed upon to accept the responsibility of becoming the principals of Mount Royal College."

[11] John Howse, *A History of Mount Royal College*, Chapter V, p. 3.

At the College, Emily developed the Mount Royal Educational Club from an idea that had originated in eastern Canada as a Ladies' Aid Society campaign. The objective of the club was to encourage reading, intellectual inquiry and spiritual growth among the young women.

The enterprise drew female students together, no matter what class or cultural background, and created a forum in which young women could develop academic presentation and public speaking skills. Students researched topics of national, international and social interest and presented their work to the group on a monthly basis. Membership was restricted to 65 female students, and each year the club would present a scholarship to a girl in financial need. The club was directed by Emily and twice was co-directed by Nellie McClung.[12] To this day, the Mount Royal Educational Club continues to function, although its membership is small and mostly elderly.

THE CALGARY LOCAL COUNCIL OF WOMEN (CLCW)

In 1912 Henrietta Muir Edwards, a prominent social activist and also vice president of the National Council of Women of Canada (NCWC), arrived in Calgary and re-instituted the defunct CLCW.[13] Fifty women formed the new Council, including Alice Jamieson as president and Emily Spencer Kerby as first vice president.

Early in the new Council Emily began to demonstrate her considerable political savvy and campaign abilities. In December 1912 she chaired the Women's Forum, dedicated to rekindling the voting interest of Calgarian women who had held the right to vote in civic elections since 1894.[14] The Civic Committee of the Council

---

[12] GAA, Mount Royal Educational Club (MREC), file M846, Miscellaneous papers.

[13] Marjorie Norris, *A Leaven of Ladies: A History of the Calgary Local Council of Women* (Calgary: Detselig, 1995), p. 38. The Council was disbanded in 1897-98.

[14] Voter interest in municipal elections had historically been very low, but it was noted that female participation was becoming increasingly apathetic. There had been some discussion among City aldermen that women's civic franchise should be rescinded. The CLCW campaigned to increase female participation to demonstrate the power of the female vote. This campaign, however, had other much broader motives as the CLCW rallied women around the prospect of a female franchise in Alberta, which would begin in earnest in 1914.

encouraged women's participation in the forum, and the press reported that Mrs. Kerby was a keen debater and a clear supporter of women's rights. On December 12, the *Morning Albertan* reported that voter representation in the December 9 civic election was the largest in the history of the City of Calgary.[15] From 1913 to 1923, Emily also served as convenor of immigration for the CLCW. Reflecting an Anglo-Saxon bias, she reported on Canada's lax immigration policies, the number of British domestics, British widows and children coming to Canada, and the number of enemy aliens interned.[16] Although she held this bias throughout her life, she maintained a practical approach to immigration and to the enrichment of Canadian life. Her reports document the broader campaigns conducted by the CLCW to Canadianize and support immigrants by providing adequate schooling for the children in rural areas, care for the indigent, transitory population, and for the mentally ill.[17]

As Convenor of Immigration, Emily campaigned to prevent child marriages among immigrant girls. Among Ukranians, also known as Austrians and Galicians, young girls were commonly married as early as age 12. The practice, Emily believed, was harmful emotionally and educationally as it limited the girls' exposure to Canadian culture, restricted the socialization process, and hampered their ability to learn English, thus retarding "Canadianization." In 1913, as vice president, she requested that the legal marriage age be raised from 18 to 21, observing that, in these communities, it was often considered a disgrace if, by the age of 15, a girl was "not married and the mother of one or two children."[18] Her petition, however, was defeated by a vote of nine to eight within the CLCW, and she was unable to proceed further with her campaign for legislation. Although Emily tried to introduce support and some protection for young women, it was not until 1917 that the Woman's Christian Temperance Union (WCTU)

---

[15] "Candidates Raked by Merciless fire of Cross Questioning by Women," *Morning Albertan*, December 12, 1912, p. 1.
[16] GAA, M.1703, Box 3, File 24, Minutes of the Executive Meeting of the CLCW, January 20, 1922.
[17] Unfortunately, this concern for the care and protection of the mentally ill, and those in society who might be harmed by these people, later expanded into a call for sterilization.
[18] Marjorie Norris, *A Leaven of Ladies*, p. 86.

actually sent a social worker to work with the Ukrainian women in Northern Alberta.[19]

Emily was an official spokesperson for the CLCW, and a gifted speaker. On June 27, 1913, she addressed the Calgary Women's Canadian Club (CWCC), not only as vice president of the Council but also as a founding member. She advocated the admittance of British and American immigrant women into the club, and of women of "colour" from India.[20] The *Calgary News-Telegram* credited her with an inspiring and persuasive presentation that won the day.

In 1914 Emily was again involved in political issues, this time for the provincial franchise for women. As Convenor for the CLCW Franchise Committee, she addressed the Council's Annual Meeting in January, 1914. Discussing the stock arguments against the franchise, she dismissed the idea that granting the vote would make women less feminine. Men put women on pedestals in order to protect them, she said, but they had no qualms about dragging women from those elevated positions of respect at any time.[21] In October that year, Emily was one of a fifteen member delegation of men and women who personally presented a petition of 44,000 signatures to Premier Arthur Sifton requesting the franchise for women. Emily, together with Mrs. Alice Jamieson, the first female magistrate appointed for Calgary, and Mrs. Annie Langford, representing the WCTU, met privately with Sifton to present the claim. However, it was not until two years later, after extensive campaigning by a persuasive network of women's organizations and trades groups, that the franchise was gained for women in March 1916. When the final date was fixed for the passing of the suffrage bill, Sifton contacted Emily personally to inform her of the details.

As Convenor of the CLCW Franchise Committee, Emily helped organize a large delegation of women from southern Alberta to attend the final reading of the bill. Two other prominent Calgary women also worked alongside Emily in the planning of this strategic visit to the Legislature. These were Jean Grant, editor of the

---

[19] Nellie McClung, "What the Women of Alberta are Doing and Saying," *Woman's Century*, December 17, 1917, p. 17.
[20] "Foreign Women Admitted to Canadian Club," *Calgary News-Telegram*, June 27, 1913, n.p.
[21] "Council of Women Out for Franchise: Past Year Saw Important Work Done," *Morning Albertan*, January 24, 1914, p. 9.

National Council of Women Convention, Calgary, 1921.
Emily Spencer Kerby is possibly on the extreme right, third row up. GAA, NA 4875-1.

women's page of the *Calgary Herald*, and Alice Jamieson. The delegation travelled to Edmonton on the Canadian Pacific Railway, and on Thursday, March 2, 1916, joined with women from Edmonton and surrounding areas to witness the passing of the franchise bill in the Legislative Assembly of Alberta.[22]

In 1916 Nellie McClung, now living in Alberta, launched a federal franchise petition. As president of the CLCW in 1916-1917, Emily and the Local Council ably assisted her, and on May 24, 1918, Canadian women achieved suffrage at the national level.

Still, the cause faced other difficulties, especially regarding women's status under the British North America Act (BNA Act), which did not seem to recognize women at all. The problem was publicly aired when the first two female Police Magistrates, Emily Murphy (Edmonton - 1916) and Alice Jamieson (Calgary - 1917), were appointed to the Bench, and several lawyers argued that they were non-persons under the BNA Act, and therefore could not preside in a court of law.[23]

Prominent social activists from the Federated Women's Institutes (FWIC), the WCTU, and the NCWC turned to the matter of women's legal status under the laws of Canada. As a focal point, they showed how women as "non-persons" were excluded from the Canadian Senate. Senators were male and scarcely conscious of the social discrimination against women, and they represented the old order at its worst.

Emily first favoured the outright abolition of the Senate, then, relenting, she called for one invigorated by women, and with an equal number of males and females. The presence of females, she declared, would facilitate moral and legal reforms.[24]

The national campaign for the recognition of women as persons under the BNA Act lasted eight years. After a series of petitions generated by the WCTU and the FWIC, together with lobbying from the NCWC, five Alberta women, later known as the Famous Five, petitioned the government for clarification regarding the constitutionality of appointing a female to the Senate of Canada. Their matter was heard before the Supreme Court of Canada in 1928, in what is now known as "The Persons Case." The highest

---

[22] "Alberta Women Hear Reading of The Woman's Suffrage Bill," *Calgary News-Telegram*, March 2, 1916, p. 13.
[23] There were other arguments regarding the lack of legal training the women had, but men, too, were often appointed without such training.
[24] Marjorie Norris, *A Leaven of Ladies*, p. 111.

court in Canada ruled that women were not persons under the strict interpretation of the BNA Act and were therefore ineligible for appointment to the Senate. In 1929 the five women, now assisted by the Attorney General of Alberta and the Canadian Government, appealed the decision to the Judicial Committee of the British Privy Council. On October 18, 1929, women (apart from Chinese and Aboriginal) became persons and were eligible for appointment to the Senate.[25]

RELIGIOUS BELIEF, WOMEN'S EQUALITY AND FAITH

Emily's interests were not, however, limited to the secular life. As a deeply religious person who was also a social reformer, she frequently and openly criticized the Christian church, especially the Methodist and later United Church traditions. This on-going critique spanned more than fifteen years, from roughly 1913 to 1928. Quoting a popular scripture verse used by many female social activists of the time (Galatians 3:28), she claimed female equality, the right to equal membership in the church, and the right for women to be ordained as ministers. The verse read, "There is no longer Jew or Greek, there is no longer slave or free, there is no longer male and female; for all of you are one in Christ Jesus." On that basis of faith, she castigated the church for its prejudice against women in making them always subservient, second-class members. In her most aggressive mood, she vehemently derided the stance of the Rev. Ernest Thomas, a prominent member of the United Church of Canada, who opposed the full ordination of women.

There was, however, a very soft and caring side to Emily's belief system. In a statement of faith which she entitled "My Creed" (c. 1920s), her warmth, compassion, intellect and social awareness were very apparent. The creed was a practical affirmation of life lived through a positive faith. She believed in the presence of God demonstrated in a mother's love, and in a nurturing community that treated others with respect, and that based itself on Christ's example. In Emily's ideal world, there was no war, no plague, no famine, just the goodness of God changing savagery into civility.

---

[25] Anne White, "The Persons Case, 1929: A Legal Definition of Women as Persons," in Sharon A. Cook, Lorna R. McLean, Kate O'Rourke, eds., *Framing Our Past: Canadian Women's History in the Twentieth Century* (Montreal-Kingston: McGill-Queen's University Press, 2001), p. 216.

It was a simple statement of belief, conveying a gentleness not often apparent in her other writings.

LATER LIFE

From 1929 until her death nine years later, Emily continued to write and publish. In 1935, under the pseudonym Constance Lynn or Lynd, she wrote one of her most aggressive and clearly feminist articles. In "Man, Woman and Freedom," she reflected on the inequalities suffered by women throughout the world over the centuries, and on how women's dream of freedom was unrealized. She was nonetheless encouraged by the advancements of women in preceding decades, and she looked forward to their future achievements and genuine freedom. Emily passionately believed that equality and freedom would one day arrive.

Emily Spencer Kerby, c. mid 1920s. PAA, 75.387/6036.

CHAPTER ONE

THE ALBERTA CONTEXT

*Between 1917 and 1927, Emily Spencer Kerby spoke as an Albertan
and a Calgarian. Writing under her preferred pseudonym, Constance
Lynd, and also as Mrs. G. W. Kerby, she challenged women to reform
society, to uphold cherished values, and to demand equality. Further, as a
member of the Christian church, she documented its early years in Calgary.*

"DAINTY PIECE OF HUMANITY"[1]

Sir Harold Bowden, English business man, says in the London
Daily Chronicle: "There is no post in the business world, or indeed
in public life, which the right woman could not fill every bit as
ably as a man."

It was the year 1917 — the Great War was in progress. Recruit-
ing had fallen to a low ebb. People were wearied by the long campaign, which seemed to have no end, when into one of our Western cities — Calgary, Alberta, stepped a tiny woman, highly educated, a beautiful voice, and dainty as a flower in her manner and
appearance.

A building was sought for her that she might speak to the citizens. Two well known women of that city set out in search of the
same. The Grand Theatre was in use; the church in the heart of the
place was in process of reconstruction after the fire which had
gutted it. What were they to do?

Incidentally, they met one of their well known men, who asked
them, "What are you two doing?" "We are looking for a building
large enough in which Mrs. Pankhurst may speak."

Looking at them with an air of disdain, he replied, "Get one of
the little rooms under the Public Library, in the basement; it will
hold everyone who will go to hear that woman."

---

[1] PAA, 75.387 (UCCA-AC), Box 181, Item 6027, Constance Lynd, "A Triumph for Womanhood," c. 1930.

Not daunted by the opinion of the man as to the audience, they succeeded in securing a large church farther out.

The evening came. Long before the hour for opening the doors, crowds filled every entrance, and away to the car lines.

As the doors opened, the ladies who had been appointed to take up a collection to defray the expenses were swept off their feet, and carried by the surging crowd from their positions. In they poured, standing in the aisles, sitting on the arms of the pews, on the steps, until every available corner was occupied.

For one and one half hours, this dainty piece of humanity (though a woman) held her audience spellbound as she told of the conditions in England at the outbreak of hostilities. Not a person left the building, although many stood throughout the whole address.

She told of England's unpreparedness in her perfect assurance of peace between Germany and the British Empire, of the condition of our first men sent to the front. Their lack of clothing, boots, ammunition, guns, and everything which went to make up a well equipped army.

She told of how the Woman's Suffrage Organization took hold of affairs, jumped into the breach, manned places of business, that the men might be released for service.

She told of how these women so despised had driven the "trams," acted as policemen — "the only woman's organization in London capable at a moment's call to get right down to work." "England," she said, "has not, nor had not the women's clubs of this land." With breathless interest, that huge throng listened to the end — leaving the church in subdued silence, as they realized England's need for more men, as never before.

Outside stood another audience, for it was warm weather. Cries of "Speech! Speech!" rang through the evening air, from hundreds of lusty throats.

Once more she took the stand in the park, and for half an hour, she talked as only a woman can, who has lived the scenes she described, pleading for help, for the wearied men at the front. In fact, it was her mission to tell to America the real truths of the war. Men who had despised her in the days of peace used her gladly in times of stress.

"The finest thing we ever heard!" "The eloquence, the masterly handling of her subject, the perfect womanliness of it all!" "She is surely God's instrument," were the comments.

That woman who had been so despised by the unthinking men and women of her day — who did not know the real heart of Mrs.

Pankhurst before, who thought only of "rotten eggs," "the burning of pillar boxes," and a general rowdy commotion, did not understand that she was fighting the greatest battle of the world — "The Emancipation of Woman," which today has spread to India, Turkey, and the countries of the Far East.

These men and women, on whose souls was dawning for the first time the greatness of the woman, went to their homes admiringly, thoughtfully, quietly, touched to the very depths of their being. As she stepped into the waiting car and was whisked from the sound of the cheering crowd to her hotel, one woman said, "Someday the people of England will build a monument to her memory in London." Though she was not a prophet, it has come true.

See! "The Times" Magazine:

"God fearing Stanley Baldwin, Prime Minister of Great Britain, who once denounced the late Mrs. Emmeline Pankhurst as an 'unnatural woman,' repented last week." When asked if he would unveil a bronze cast of "Suffragette Pankhurst" — subscriptions for which are now being solicited, [he] said, "I will."

"Appropriately, Big-Little Mrs. Pankhurst is cast seven feet tall; and stands on a four foot pedestal in the corridor of the House of Parliament, towering triumphantly above the minute males."

The world has always crucified its great reformers, its saints, its saviours. What pain and suffering she might have been saved [from] had common sense prevailed.

The work she did has spread to the outermost confines of the world. The educated women of India, of Turkey, of Japan, are being "called" to places of public trust — but our Canada lags far behind in its appreciation of her women.

Yet they have been the backbone of the country, they have borne the burden and heat of the day, equally with men, and at the eventide, yet have not received their "penny"of recognition from its government, its voters, or its churches.

"DON'T TALK OF SUCH THINGS"[2]

What is the matter with our civilization: Alberta is under the old North West Territories Act and governed by old English laws of some 300 years past.

Just fancy; in this twentieth century, "a man may procure a

[2] Constance Lynd, "Laws — Equal Justice," Alberta Section - Editorial Comment, *Woman's Century*, November 1919, p. 49.

divorce from his wife for adultery, but a woman may not divorce her husband, save as she can *prove* adultery and ill-usage."

Oh, ye gods! This is Canada, and women are citizens; and men and woman are equal (?)

Just here, how would it do to have a plank in our Woman's platform:

Equal pay for equal work,

Equal punishment for equal crime.

Also how would it be to make adultery a crime, all over Canada. Sh-sh — don't talk of such things — the men will not like it.

"WHAT ARE WE COMING TO!"[3]

Surely the West is progressive. Calgary is the proud possessor of a "Cat Club."

When it was first talked of we thought it a joke; in fact, gave it very little consideration, supposing it was a term of disdain applied to our women's organizations because of women daring to express their opinions.

Of course, if women do this and get ruffled, we are called "cats." If men do likewise, and get not only "ruffled" but hot in defence of their ideas, they are "lions."

So we really have a "Cat Club," not women, but the genuine "me-yow" kind that express their opinions nightly, not only to the "listening moon," but to the would-be tired being who fain is compelled to listen. Yes, a "Cat Club," to discuss the menu for cats — the proper feeding of baby cats, as the mortality among them is so appalling — often in families of four or five little ones, all die save one. Canada must arouse herself to this abused branch of her citizens. What an awful row there will be when the "Cat Club" and the "Dog Club" hold their annual convention.

Then there are many cats without homes. These must be adopted into respectable families where they'll be cared for as their own.

Soon we'll have "cats' policemen," and a juvenile cats' court to decide the nightly rows under humans' windows, and who should be fined for the bricks and boots, etc., hurled from windows, disturbing the night concerts and evening revelries.

What are we coming to when in this period of seriousness, this period of readjustment — when men, women and children need our best thought, care, and service, to turn it upon cats.

---

[3] Constance Lynd, "Cat Club," *Women's Century*, January, 1920, p. 43.

"EIGHTEEN MONTHS FOR A RUINED LIFE"[4]

A mother and father in a country district desirous of getting proper education for their daughter, a girl of thirteen years, put her in charge of a man friend of thirty-three years of age, to take her to a certain city, "get her a boarding house and let her go to school."

She reached the city. He took her to a hotel, kept her there for some days, registered as his wife.

Today he is in the penitentiary, and she is in the Social Service home.

Will mothers never learn the dangers of such a course? God gave you that child, and He expects you to care for her. What is eighteen months in prison? It should be eighteen years. Seven years for stealing a cow — eighteen months for a ruined life! Our lives are all wrong. Women arouse yourselves and see to it that these vampires get their deserts. Nothing but floggings, and long term imprisonments (and maybe the surgeon's knife) will be the effectual means of checking such crimes.

"HIGH IDEALS"[5]

Women of the Canadian Club: We come to the beginning of another year.[6] I wish for you all that it may be a happy one. I've been wondering what is our outlook for 1925. The past year has gone — for weal or woe, we cannot recall it. Let us look ahead.

Here are some words of hope for Canadians. Canada's dollar is the only currency in the world quoted as a premium above the United States dollar since the war.

The name of Canada stands high throughout the world. Her credit is excellent. Her resources and natural advantages are great. She is producing a fine, sturdy, upstanding race of excellent men and women.

To be a Canadian is an excellent trademark everywhere. The greatness of Canada's future is beyond question. But I wish to turn to another side. The most important one: Have we, as a Canadian Club, the high ideals we should have for our country?

---

[4] Constance Lynd, "Mothers Think!" *Woman's Century*, January 1920, p. 43.
[5] "Calgary Women's Practical Work ... With an Address by Mrs. G. W. Kerby, Retiring President," *The Maple Leaf*, February 1925, p. 28.
[6] Emily was then the retiring president of the Women's Canadian Club. She was listed in the new 1925 executive as vice president.

Have we that "passionate patriotism" heard recently that Canada needs — are we seeing visions and dreaming dreams for her, to be later put into concrete form?

Have we any definite ideals for her future, and [are we] aiming towards it, or are we simply drifting, with no sense of our obligation to this land of our birth or adoption?

For many generations in Holland the dykes have been an essential factor in the safety and prosperity of the country. The greatest care and supervision is given to these lest there should be a leak, and so life and property be lost, with the incoming of the sea over the low lands.

You may be surprised to know that Canada has her dykes. They are not visible to the human eye, but are more important than the dykes of Holland.

The first dyke I wish to speak of is our Canadian Christian Sabbath. This is one of the beneficent gifts to man. The nations of the world are beginning to realize its importance, and their need of it.

China needs this dyke to protect childhood. In one factory alone we are told 1,100 little boys are employed from 4 a.m. to 6:30 p.m., seven days a week — at 25 cents a day. What hope for a nation bereft of its day of rest?

I do not believe [in] or ask for the old Puritanical Sabbath, but I ask as members of the Canadian Club that we hold this dyke. It is leaking.

The next dyke I wish to speak of is the Christian Home. Here it is (and nowhere else can it be done) that children must and should learn from their parents, the first principles of truthfulness, honesty, purity and their responsibility to God.

"Give me the child till he is 9 years of age," it has been said, "and I care not who has him after." That means the home. These are the years, where of necessity, the child is closely allied with his parents and his home.

This dyke is leaking seriously, and if we are to maintain our reputation as Canadians for honesty and integrity we must hold the dyke.

The third and last of which I will speak is the dyke of Christian Marriage.

Some time ago, [while I was] sitting beside a well known gentleman, he made this remark, "Well, you know Mrs. Kerby, we are seeing now the last of marriage — we shall return to the promiscuous life — children will be brought up in institutions."

6

I looked at him feeling there was a serious leak in his dyke. Did he not know we are only emerging from the "promiscuous" and from polygamy? We are on the way out. Not back. When India and Turkey are beginning to adopt our Christian ideals it is no time for Canadian men to talk of moving backward.

All over our land, men and women are living together as man and wife, with no Christian or legal sanctification of their relationship. Why? Because we have no law to make it a crime. You can't touch it. But as members of the Canadian Club, we must touch it. The dyke is leaking, and endangering our whole people.

Dyke holding is pre-eminently the work of Canadian Clubs. We must hold them for the sake of the on-coming generations. Do you see them? Can you hear the patter, patter of little feet, stretching away into the distance?

I am a great believer in the progress or evolution of the race. Aren't you?

We are strange creatures, so few of us take the long look. Too few of us catch the vision or follow the gleam. Years ago, when Tennyson wrote those wonderful lines depicting the future navigation of the air — people laughed. Listen!

> For I dipt into the future, far as human eye could see,
> Saw the vision of the world, and all the wonders that would be;
> Saw the heavens fill with commerce argosies of mighty sail;
> Pilots of the purple twilight, dropping down their costly bales,
> Heard the heavens fill with shouting, and there rained a ghastly dew
> Of the nations' airy navies grappling in the central blue.

People laughed, and said it can never be, but the aeroplane came.

Even as Tennyson saw years before its time the navigation of the air, so another poet has caught the vision of the new race which will arrive, not as a cataclysm, but as a gradual development. Can we too not get a view of it as well?

> This shall be a loftier race
> Than ere the world hath known shall rise.
> With flame of freedom in their souls,
> And light of knowledge in their eyes.

They shall be gentle, brave and strong
To spill no drop of blood, but dare
All that may plant man's lordship firm
On earth and fire, on sea and air.

Nation with nation, land with land
Unarmed shall live as comrades free,
And every heart and brain shall throb
With pulse of one fraternity.

- J. A. Symonds.[7]

Did you ever think that Paul saw it when he urged the people of his day to strive on, "Till they came to the perfect likeness of God in Christ"?

And it is coming. We're nearer it today than ever before. Then why not in Canada, the first home of the New Race? Why shall we not be the first to evolve to the heights here described?

Canada! Our Canada!
"Last born of Nations, the offspring of freedom,
Heir to wide prairies, rich forest, red gold.
God give us wisdom to value our birthright,
Courage to guard what we hold."[8]

Isn't it worth holding the dykes when we have such a goal? It's worth not only putting in our fingers to stop the leak, but our arm, and our body and soul, if need be, for Canada's sake, and for future Canadians.

"CHURCH HISTORY IN CALGARY"[9]

Upon this occasion of the celebration of the jubilee of Canada's Confederation it is as well to regard for a time the work of the churches. Have they kept apace with the growth of its population, its business, and the rapid strides of industry? Have they paralleled

---

[7] John Addington Symonds (1840-1893) was a British writer and poet. He composed these verses as a hymn. Emily was particularly fond of these verses and quoted them frequently in her writings and speeches.
[8] Emily appears to be quoting one of her own compositions here.
[9] PAA, 75.387, Box 181, Item 6027, Mrs. G.W. Kerby, "Calgary's Churches Have Developed With Inspiring Rapidity," n.d.

with the education work and general development of our fair city? We shall see.

The opening of church history in Calgary begins with the little log church erected in the late Dr. McDougal's time, in June 1877. It was located beside the first Mounted Police barracks at Sixth Street East.

The year 1883 brought great changes to the tiny hamlet nestling in the valley of the Bow River. Men began to arrive in the country, eager to become located "ahead of steel" that to some extent at least they might have a foothold in this country before the great trans-continental railway should arrive.[10]

There were no services being held in the log church by the barracks at this time. These men from the eastern part of our country had always been used to having a church to attend. The log church was across the Elbow River, and they were east of it. A church they must have, and they set themselves the task of erecting one in that locality, this spot being the nucleus of the present city — called then — Fort Calgary.

Under the direction and assistance of Hon. W. H. Cushing, still resident in our midst, the first church in Calgary was erected: a very humble one indeed, made of boards half way up the side, and completed with a tent roof.[11] It was opened under the aegis of the Methodist church, and a minister [was] appointed, in the person of Rev. James Turner. This church later was replaced by another, on the west side of the river.

There must have been some foreshadowing of the future in what resulted; for the Methodists used it in the morning, and the Presbyterians in the evening.[12] That autumn witnessed the arrival of the Catholics and Anglicans.

Other small churches arose; primitive indeed as was the first, but with plenty of room to grow; and grow they did, some of them being enlarged two and three times. Later the Baptists erected their first place of worship, at the corner of Sixth Avenue and Second

---

[10] Emily was a strong feminist, and she insisted that women be included in the written history of Canada. It is ironic that she would use the term "men" when describing both men's and women's contribution.

[11] W. H. Cushing was a Calgary Member of the Provincial Parliament, an MPP, known today as an MLA. He was also the first Alberta Minister of Public Works.

[12] The Presbyterians and Methodists were amalgamated into the United Church of Canada in 1925.

Street West. The building still stands, occupied by another group of people.[13]

In 1890, the Salvation Army arrived, beginning work which has grown with the years.

The year 1903 saw the whole religious field manned by these five denominations, for a city of about 6,000 persons.[14]

The gradual, but steady growth of the place had made it imperative that the old churches should be abandoned and new ones substituted. The then Methodist church had thrown off its dress of logs, wood and shingles, and had become arrayed in perfectly good bricks; quite pretentious for that era. This building is now the Arlington Hotel, on Sixth Avenue and Second Street West. The Presbyterians were housed in a fine structure of Calgary sandstone on the corner of Centre Street and Seventh Avenue, where at present exists only a deep hole surrounded by a high fence.

The Catholic church was in its present position, in the "Missions" as it was always called then.[15] The Anglican Pre-cathedral stood on the same site as at present on the corner of Seventh Avenue and First Street.

This provided five churches, and the Salvation Army to do the religious work at the time, for a city of 6,000 people. It will be interesting to observe how it compared with today.

Here dwelt a thoroughly contented and church going community. Each Sabbath saw these churches thronged with the inhabitants of the city as well from the ranches around about, for there were few indeed of such places, save in the villages widely scattered on the foothills. At that time there was far more vacant than occupied land in the province.

The next few years saw that great influx of population. Peoples from all over the eastern part of Canada and from the old

---

[13] First Baptist Church was organized in 1888, and its members met in the Masonic Hall on 8th Avenue S.E. The first chapel was erected in 1890, on 6th Avenue and 2nd Street S.W.

[14] Emily mentions five denominations, yet there were at least seven, including the Moravians and the Salvation Army. The Salvation Army did not present itself as an official denomination but as a religious organization outside of denominational categories. The Salvationists considered themselves a soul-winning army.

[15] The first Roman Catholic mission in Calgary was built by the Oblate Fathers in the Mission District in the early 1870s. The first Methodist and Anglican churches were built in Calgary in 1884.

land came, desiring to make their homes in what appeared small indeed, yet was destined to be the beautiful "City of the Foothills." The churches could not hold the people, and great accommodation was urgently required. The Methodist church was the first to attempt a more commodious place of gathering. After worshiping in what was known as Hull's Opera House, on Centre Street, for a year and a half, they had the joy of seeing the present building on First Street West completed and ready for opening in February 1905. It was a great event, to the early settlers here, to see such a building. This was named Central Methodist Church.

Shortly afterward the Baptist church followed the lead, putting up a very pretty edifice, across the street from Central, on the property now occupied by the Herald building.

The spirit of enlargement came to the Presbyterians, the same necessity driving them to enlarge their borders. This church, a stone building... situated on Seventh Avenue, was too good a location at that time to depart from. It was central. The building was remodeled on the site where it stood by enlarging the church proper, and building a new schoolroom because the Sabbath schools were growing so very rapidly, and space for their work was emergent.

During the time of rebuilding they betook themselves for worship to the "Lyric Theatre" — afterwards called the "Pantages Theatre," now the "Arcade."

In the midst of all this change, the Baptist church, a frame structure, caught fire and burned to the ground in spite of the valiant efforts of the efficient firemen. It was a bitter night, one of the coldest ever seen in our city. When morning dawned, there was as pretty sight as one could wish to see; a palace of glittering ice, tinted with every shade and colour of the rainbow, as the sun played in brilliant splendour over the ruins of the previous night.

Nothing undaunted by their loss, they proceeded to clear the land, and when a long-looked for Chinook arrived, they were soon ready to begin the work of the new and better building — later moving to their present situation on Thirteenth Avenue and Fourth Street West, as central property became too valuable to hold, and they too required a larger place of worship. Knox now erected the beautiful cathedral-like church on the corner of Fourth Street and Sixth Avenue West. The Anglican and Catholic churches were each enlarged on their present locations.

But a change came. It was no longer the enlarging of the edifices to cope with the rapidly growing city which was spreading in every direction. In 1903 the city was practically confined within the bounds of Fourth Streets, west and east, and from Fifteenth Avenue to the Bow River. By 1908 the city had spread from these confines to what is now Hillhurst and Sunnyside [and] from Mount Royal and Sunalta to Crescent Heights. East Calgary, too, began to make itself known. The "Mission" enlarged, while shadows of Ogden were in the offing as well as the beauty spot of Elbow Park.

The ministers who represented these different churches worked hard and long. They held services and Sunday schools in different parts of the city to assist in reaching the outermost parts, with its newly arrived citizens.

These were not the days of everybody having a motor car. The street railway was only in process of construction. To the churches, this resulted in a period of expansion; not the rebuilding and enlarging of the past, but the erecting of new churches in the strategic points in every part of the rapidly extending areas of the city's far-reaching borders. The older people needed a church, and the children a place for Sunday schools. This change accounts for the original denominations in the outermost bounds of the city.

The then Methodist church, began by building Wesley, followed by Trinity and Crescent Heights. The Presbyterians came along with Grace, St. Andrews, and in Hillhurst. The Baptists opened in several points, and the Anglicans built in East Calgary, Crescent Heights, St. Stephens and others.

The Catholic church was not one whit behind in its early extension, in each new section opened up to residents.

The work did not end here. On and on it went, until in our city today are found the greatest number of not only useful, but pretty modern places of worship that it has been the privilege of any place as young as Calgary to possess.

Sometimes it is a cause for wonder where all the money came from to erect these structures which dot the whole of the city. Surely it is a tribute to the people that amidst the building of a city, their business, and their homes, they did not forget the higher and spiritual things which are indicated by these structures. Great changes have taken place, even in the quiet days of the war, and since, when there was almost no extension of this work. The union of three large denominations was consummated — in the United Church of Canada.

To the credit of the following churches we find that the Anglican, Baptist, Presbyterian, Catholic and United Church of Canada have some 40 edifices. The Salvation Army has seven places, seeking to do its best for humanity. Besides these, recent years have seen many new communities of worship opened. Among them are the Lutheran, the Jewish synagogues, the Church of Christ, the Pentecostal church, the Nazarenes, the Christian Science and other smaller ones held in halls and club rooms, making in all more than 50 places of worship for the residents and strangers coming to visit us. In which they may find food for their spiritual needs.

Now a new idea has come to the hearts of our citizens, and Central United has the honour of leading with its set of chimes, thanks to the generosity of one of our citizens, Hon. R. B. Bennett, K.C., LL.D., M.P.[16]

To retain the sequence of events, Knox should follow with its chimes. Then the Anglican (which we hear are already arranged for, through the thoughtfulness of the late W. R. Hull).[17] Then should come the Catholics and Baptists with theirs, to greet with their music the Sabbath morn, calling to worship every citizen of our city.

Today we find upward of 50 places of worship, of various kinds and creeds, for a population of approximately 75,000.

Has the church done her duty in our city? We leave you to draw your own conclusions.

In giving the review of the various churches it would not be complete without mentioning three pioneer men, who in the very early days devoted their lives to the bringing of the gospel to this western country, particularly southern Alberta.

We first think of Father Lacombe, who laboured unceasingly to bring to the Indians the gospel of Christ. We do not enumerate: the mere mention of his name brings sweet memories to hundreds. The town of Lacombe, and the Lacombe Home, near Midnapore, are the monuments to his devotion. While Alberta lasts, this name will ever be in her memory.

---

[16] Richard Bedford Bennett was a prominent CPR solicitor in the West. In 1909 he was elected as a Conservative MPP. In 1911 he was elected to the House of Commons. In 1927 the Conservative party held its first leadership convention, and Bennett was elected leader. In 1930 he became Prime Minister of Canada, but in 1935 he was defeated.

[17] Richard Roper Hull was one of Calgary's most prominent businessmen, having started in the ranching business in 1884, and later expanding into meatpacking. He was one of the founders of the Calgary Brewing & Malting Company.

The results of Rev. Dr. John McDougall's long service are seen in the lifting of our Indians to a higher and more civilized life. He saw them changed from the wild savage hunters and fighters, who knew no law but the law of the jungle, to law-abiding peaceful, industrious men, tilling the soil and educating their children. His memory will ever be green in the memory of the Indian tribes with whom he came in contact — a man beloved by them all. He was, in word and deed, their friend. He was endowed with wonderful ability to gain the confidence of the tribes, and what he has saved the government of this country in men and money in being able to quell by peaceful methods the early uprisings will never be known.

On Dominion Day a cairn will be unveiled at Morley to his memory, he having for many years resided there.

One other must not go unmentioned: Rt. Rev. Dr. Pinkham, formerly [Anglican] Bishop of Calgary, who is still with us, after long years of service. He is a well known figure on our city streets, in its councils and community work. Though the shadows of the evening of life have fallen, he is yet keenly interested in all things pertaining to the welfare of the community. He has helped in the city's making; and to him is the reward of a well earned rest.

"AFFORDABLE VACATIONS FOR WOMEN AND GIRLS"[18]

It was never intended, not yet thought of when they started it now some sixteen years ago. The only thought of these women was to provide a safe and homelike place for the rapidly increasing class of young ladies coming to this Western country, to have a rea-sonably cheap place of abode in our wonderful mountains, which form the natural barrier between Alberta and British Columbia.[19]

These women lived in that rapidly growing city of Calgary. True, there were lakes, and lakes where a pleasant holiday might be spent, but no access to them, no place of abode for them, and no sources of supplies.

There was, however, a railroad to the Rocky Mountains, built by that pathfinder, developer and safeguarder of the Western plains, the Canadian Pacific Railroad Company. A corporation to

[18] PAA, 75.387 (UCCA-AC), Box 181, Item 6028, Constance Lynd, "What Women Have Done, Women Can Do," c. 1923.

[19] The women were the Directors and founders of the Calgary YWCA, an organization that also included the board of the Travellers' Aid Society.

which Canada, and perhaps Western Canada in particular, owes more than she can ever repay. Only men of vision and faith could have planned, completed, and managed such an undertaking successfully. Those who say aught else speak ignorantly.

Ninety miles from Calgary were the glorious Rocky Mountains. People from all over the world came to visit the scene, and enjoy their beauty. But it took money, far beyond the ability of the average woman, to stay at these places, and the then few hotels in these mountain resorts.

Why should not the women and girls of our city and province be able to likewise enjoy the scenery? This was the question asked by these women of Calgary. The question bore fruit in the form of renting a house and providing tent houses on the grounds, where the girls of the community could be taken care of in safety.[20]

Later, a property was bought on which was a very lovely bungalow; tents and tent houses covered the grounds, until a sudden vision dawned on these women as to what might be done in the future, if only they could persuade the rest that their vision was not a mirage.

The years passed, not without anxiety; the house was remodeled, additions made year by year, until at this present time we have a beautiful Chalet, operated by the Young Woman's Christian Association, accommodating ninety-six guests. A dining room seating fifty-five at a time, a beautiful rotunda, some forty feet square; and all presided over by a General Secretary and a staff of assistants.

Then the men of more humble means, coming with their wives, asked that they might be taken in as well. They came, and we arranged our house for their comfort and convenience that there should be no discrimination.

The years passed, and the vision grew. Another Chalet was erected at Lake Louise, with a capacity of fifty-five guests, in perfect comfort. Here too, a competent Secretary and a staff of assistants work[ed] through the summer or tourist season for the welfare and enjoyment of their guests.

Then why not have a place at Field? — that "spot on top of the world" as someone has called it. Here now is a building with a capacity of forty guests.

Here in the very heart of the Rockies, these women, a Board of seven, have acquired, managed, and consolidated under the aegis

---

[20] The facilities were possibly near Banff.

of the Young Women's Christian Association, over $75 worth [$750 or $7,500] of property — by dint of sheer push, pluck, and perseverance.

Many of the married couples who visit us are the women who in past years have been workers in the Y.W.C.A. in other parts of the world. And we do have them from every corner of the globe.

What women have done, women can do. Their capacity for detail makes them eminently efficient when they banish fear. Fear is the bug-bear of womankind and will be, until they try their wings. I do not mean "angel's wings" — we were credited with for too long a time, to our very undoing; but I mean *business wings*, which are far more valuable in this work-a-day world than the former.

An amusing incident before we close. The writer of this story was in the Lake Louise Chalet — behind the desk — talking to the secretary one evening about 10 p.m., when a gentleman of some fifty years of age came up and asked, "Is it all right for my brother and I to stay here?" A laughing answer was given by our kindly Secretary, assuring that is was quite all right when we had the room, although our policy was "Ladies first."

He still hesitated, when I could not refrain from a little fun.

"Are you comfortable?"

"Oh! yes, very."

"Are you nervous?"

"No, but my brother (a man of sixty) is," he very smilingly replied.

We promised them our best protection, while with us, and I may say they stayed. While we got a great thrill that for the first time in our lives, we had the glorious sense of man's fear of woman.

The tables are turning. What may we not accomplish yet?

Emily Spencer Kerby and George Kerby, Mt. Royal College, Calgary, c. 1920.
GAA, NA 4855-9.

18

CHAPTER TWO

SOCIAL HISTORY THROUGH STORIES

Emily wove tales of intrigue, romance, courage and corruption. There were star-crossed lovers, heroic pioneers, hypocrites, adventurers, even sexual dabblers who experimented in "companionate marriages," or common law liaisons. From the romantic to the tragic, she incorporated them all into the social milieu of her writing.

YOUNG LOVE CONQUERS ALL[1]

Somehow a maddening sense of frustration had irked at intervals the tall young man, who stood restlessly watching from the window that morning the Empress of India, with her load of human freight, slowly swing into the dock. As she pulled up alongside, and the gangplank was thrown out, his interest ceased; he turned for the third time to his father's office, ostensibly on business, but in reality to ascertain if Nora Towers, his father's private secretary, were there.

Browsing the room at a glance, he exclaimed, "What is wrong? Where is Nora today?" Father Strathdore senior gazed intently a moment at his son; grim determination written plainly on his usually handsome face, while he looked disapprovingly at his son.

To add to his imperiousness, he rose, strode across the room — turned, and looking Hal straight in the eyes said, "I dismissed her."

"You dismissed her?" said the young man.

"Yes, I did," came the decisive reply, "and for a perfectly good reason of my own."

"May I ask what that reason is? And also, where has she gone? My absence from the city accounts for my ignorance."

---

[1] PAA, 75.387 (UCCA-AC), Box 181, Item 6028, Constance Lynd, "Grist," c. 1918.

The scene of this conversation was the office of Strathdore and Son, on the third floor of the Metropolitan Building, overlooking the rose blue waters of Vancouver harbour.

"Do I need to tell you, Hal, why I have dispensed with her services? Sure I have made myself perfectly plain in regard to your infatuation for the girl. Though I must say I did not realize until recently how great a hold she was gaining on your attention. Had I been doubtful before, the expression now on your face, depicts clearly your attitude of mind."

"Much as I have valued her as my secretary, she has become utterly abhorrent to me, seeing as I do so unmistakably your determined persistence in carrying out your desires. I have other plans for you, plans which I have long cherished; indeed, it has become an obsession so great that I cannot, nor will not relinquish. I have never spoken to you about them until now, save in an indefinite way, because until recently you have not shown serious predilection toward any of the girls with whom you associate. I want that the name of Strathdore may be perpetuated among Canada's greatest men — even the top round of the ladder would not be too high for that name, Hal. It's my ambition to leave a name behind me that shall live when I am gone."

Pausing a moment, he gazed at his son, as a smile of assured victory crossed his face; while meditatively he tapped his pencil on the mahogany desk, he resumed — "A marriage with Kathleen Temaire will unite these two firms among the West's oldest, and give you a most enviable place in both social and business world[s]."

A dark shadow crossed the usually happy features of the younger man. "Damn position and society! You know I care nothing for these things. The only position I crave is to be of some service to my fellow beings in this world. You forget I too have aspirations, Father, of which I have spoken freely, and which must have consideration from you. Your life has largely been lived. Mine lies in the future. Kathleen and I would be a sad misfit. She is a society girl; it is her life. That sort of thing does not appeal to me, nor ever will. We have been playmates for years, and I am just as sure that she has no such thought in regard to me. And more, I do not wish her to have any. Since this has come up in the manner it has, I can assure you it would have been better had you consulted me, your own son, before you made a decision like this."

Dull consternation melted slowly into the keen-edged understanding. The financier brought his eyes back from the restful peaks of the mountains in the distance, over which the morning sunlight hung [like] a crown of gold, as Hal stood outlined in silhouette against the window.

"Surely you knew my meaning when I talked with you of my ideas in regard to the future on this matter. You never appeared to be interested, or respond to what I had in mind; but now that I see exactly how the land lies, and you appear to ignore all my wishes, you are forcing me to find out what other means will accomplish."

Again, his eyes wandered to the mountains in the distance, which seemed to say — "Be strong as we are, and you will conquer." Yes, strong as the Lions which reared their proud heads aloft.

Hal looked at his father with a searching gaze, was about to leave the room, then turned saying, "Am I right in thinking that you, my own father, will use force to consummate your ends?"

"This is exactly what I intend to convey to you, Hal."

A troubled face looked appealingly at the older man for a moment, then set with a look of determination, which precedes a storm — "Very well, Father, if that is your line, and you put up a challenge, we'll see who wins. So far, my experience of life has told me that right always does — in the end."

Strathdore senior had never seen his son in a role such as this. "There is no doubt who will win," came ironically from his lips, amazement written unmistakably on his countenance.

A moment of indecision, Hal's face went ashen white. He pulled his watch from his pocket, turned on his heel, and strode from the room.

For himself, he felt only a rather savage exaltation. He never doubted but that success would be his; and in that moment of anticipated triumph, he was borne along as on the wings of the wind, seeing or hearing nothing, when suddenly he came face to face with the object of his thoughts.

"Why, Nora! I cannot tell you how glad I am that you have not left the city. I have been wondering what was wrong with father; he has not seemed himself lately." This remark came as she told him what had happened the previous evening.

"I could not get you on the phone, Hal, for I knew that you had gone to Victoria on business for a couple of days. I wish I had known that you returned last night. I was so taken by surprise when I received my short and curt dismissal, to 'take effect at once' with a month's salary in advance. It was my intention to go away tomorrow, only I felt I must see you before I went. Then I ran across my old friend, Mr. Greaves, of the Government Children's Aid Department. Naturally I was desperate, and before I realized what I was doing, I told him the whole story. He has always been such a friend to me. I've known him ever since I can remember. I needed someone to whom I could talk; I could not tell Gussie Trevors, where I stay; she'd have it all over the city before morning. Mr. Greaves persuaded me to come and help him for a time, until his stenographer who is very ill returns. He is fearfully behind with his work; so I have promised to assist him until then. That is where I am bound for now. Somehow, Hal, your father's office appeared to me as a permanency always. This upheaval makes me feel like a tramp. It was a staggering blow, after all these years, when he invariably expressed himself as so satisfied with me and my work. Really, I am stunned.... One thing, Hal, I have a right to know the real reason of dismissal, for I am convinced the one given was not the true one; it was that 'An old friend has asked me to take his daughter into my own office, and I feel I must grant his request.'"

[Finally, Nora concluded:] "I must talk no longer, but away to my new job."

"All right," said Hal, "I too have an appointment. Besides, the street is hardly the place to discuss this. I'll be round this evening and take you for a drive, then we can consider what is best to be done." Lifting his hat with a reassuring smile, they parted.

Meanwhile, Mr. Strathdore paced the floor of his office. "I never dreamed this thing had gone so far; but I have started, and it is not in the nature of James Strathdore to deflect from his purpose. My indomitable will and persistence has made this business. Hal has all my characteristics in this line, but perverted for the time. He'll thank me some day for what I have determined to do. Yes, of course, he is nearly twenty-seven, but even [people] that age do not always appreciate what is advantageous for them. It's all a case of propinquity. What a calamity I did not sooner see what was going on right under my eyes. I should have known that a young man of Hal's type (and it's a good type) would have naturally been attracted by such a girl. Fine looking, athletic, plays tennis and swims like a professional, and when it comes to her character, she's four square. Silent in the office when she should be, but quick as a flash to see through things, and can talk the best of sense when needed. A jewel! But what I have set my heart on must go."

Weeks had passed into months, and Nora was still in the office of her old friend, who, crossing the room, requested her to look up the files of the year regarding the adoption of a child, a ward of the

Government, by the name of Lena Strong. "A case in court, facts necessary, some property affair."

As she turned the leaves of the great file, a name caught her eye. She stopped abruptly, looked closely at the page. Flashes of carmine swept over her temples and ran upwards into her dark hair. One furtive glance round the room to assure herself she was not observed, she quickly pencilled something from the records and slipped it in her bosom.

That evening as usual, Hal called to take her round Marine Drive after a long day in the office. Besides, he wanted to arrange some definite action as soon as she was free to leave her old friend.

It was a June evening. Flowers were everywhere in profusion. Such an evening as might make those even who were not lovers rejoice in the beauty of this world.

As the car swept along, and they later entered Stanley Park, under its towering trees, and amid its ferns, he tried to talk to her but she was strangely silent. Her voice was troubled and wistful, tears seemed not far away. He drew up at the yacht club door, saying, "I am going to take you for a sail. Perhaps the sea breezes will restore your wonted gaiety."

An emerald twilight had flung her velvet mantle of mist over the sleeping water, as the cat-boat slipped from her moorings. Hal was busy bringing the boat into trim, against a light breeze which had suddenly sprung up. In a moment it caught the stronger current, and as the little craft sped further out, the sail bellied and in a short time they were speeding through the "Narrows," rocked by the roll of the waves from the ocean beyond.

From time to time Hal glanced anxiously at the girl so strangely silent, for sailing had always been such a delight to her. Tonight there was no thrill as the boat sped on.

The shadows of the evening had given place to the glorious orb of night, resplendent in all its fullness. Still, the disquieting silence prevailed, broken only by the musical lap, lap, of the water, as the trim craft rode the waves.

Not infrequently, as they cut through the picture of the old orange moon reflected on the surface of the water, did he try to draw her into conversation; but failed utterly.

He could not understand what was the matter, nor procure any clue as to the cause, the result of which caused him to renew the affair which disturbed her with his father the next day, as they two sat at the breakfast table.

"Father, may I ask you once more why you have such an aversion to Nora? She is one of the finest girls I ever knew — in fact the only one who has ever really attracted me and …."

Instantly the face of the older man changed. He had been conversing pleasantly with his son, who had mistaken his cheerful attitude as favorable to attack the problem.

Assuming a haughty air, while a settled frown clouded the recently agreeable countenance, Mr. Strathdore jerked out in a most pre-emptory manner, "Hal, never mention that girl's name to me again."

[Strathdore Sr.] rose from the table, leaving his meal unfinished as a silent protest.

Some evenings later, in response to a ring, Nora opened the door to be brought face to face with Mr. Strathdore.

Terror filled her heart, fear that in the revulsion of feeling toward him, she might betray too soon to his discerning eye the weapon she held as in the hollow of her hand. He entered without hesitation, bowed somewhat stiffly, refusing the proffered chair; then rushed headlong into the subject which so obsessed his mind.

In a few cryptic words he explained his sudden and unannounced appearance before her, saying in his most suave manner, "Only be reasonable, Miss Towers, and my business will soon be over. Then you and I need never meet again. It is a most unusual proceeding for a man in my position to call on his late discharged secretary. I am glad to find you alone," [he said, glancing] round the room, "for should it become generally known that I have been here, malicious ones might set afloat stories which would injure for the time my so far untarnished reputation; as well, it might reflect unhappily on you, though to a lesser degree. Knowing this I have ventured all in my endeavour to save my son from what I deem youthful folly."

Nora stood quietly before him. No change of expression gave the slightest hint of the thoughts rushing through her mind. She knew her hour of avengement had come. How often in the quiet of the night had she pictured it all. What she would do and what she would say when it arrived — for arrive it would.

A fearful silence ensued. Without answering him, she stepped quietly to her desk, drew forth a slip of paper, and handed it to Strathdore, who read it nonchalantly. For a moment his eyes fell. He appeared embarrassed, then recovering himself and eyeing her with a cynical smile said, "Well, what will your next move be?"

"That is my secret. One thing I do know, you shall never foist Kathleen Temaire on Hal; nor would she wish to ever bear the name of Strathdore. She has (and rightfully) a great pride of family, and further that 'untarnished reputation' of yours shall not go unsullied. Beware! One thing I must know. Were you cognizant of my identity the years I was in your office? Swear! Swear!"

Somewhat thrown off his guard, he replied, "I can solemnly swear to you that I did not know. It as a thing of the past, a forgotten dream."

Drawing herself to her full slender height, she stiffened; all the intensity of her being portrayed in her posture, she exclaimed, "A thing of the past! A forgotten dream!" Then pausing as she clenched her hands until the imprint of the nails showed plainly on the white flesh, she said, "I loathe you, and could I do so, I would …."

One glance at the man's face silenced her. Drawing his eyes into curves of concentration, he scanned her coldly a moment, then stepping toward the entrance of the room, Strathdore — his hand on the knob, half turned, and with a sneer in his voice said, "One thing has been accomplished at least. You know now that you and Hal can never marry. I am indebted to you for so excellent a solution of my difficulty." Silently as a snake, and watching Nora closely, he left the room.

The following evening the two young people were together on one of Vancouver's beautiful beaches. Again Hal endeavoured to draw the girl out of her strange reticence. At last he succeeded in getting the whole story as she crumpled up by his side.

He looked at her with an expression of infinite pity. Placing his hand in tenderness on hers, "Surely there is a way out, there must be. The fact that father made no suggestion as to your future does not appear to me a square thing. There may be more we do not know, of which we ought to have knowledge. There must be some way to solve this all" — as with troubled countenance, he gazed far out to sea, apparently lost in the vastness of not only the great ocean stretched out before him, but of the greater ocean of life.

Suddenly the young man sprang to his feet, plunging a hand into either pocket, rapidly paced the sandy beach; then as abruptly, stopped before her. "Nora, something has occurred to me. A memory of long ago. I wonder! Perhaps it may bring us light as to our future movements. I feel in view of what you have told me that I have a right (or would be perfectly justified) in doing what has suddenly come to my mind. I remember — but wait — I can at least try." In a few words he told her of a childish memory. "It may be nothing, still it is worth the effort. Something tells me that there lies the thing we must know…. May I take you home? I must do what I have to tonight; tomorrow might be too late. I cannot rest until I have made sure of the old recollection."

In almost absolute silence, the two wended their way to Nora's residence. Instead of going to his home in Point Grey, he boarded a passing street car to the centre of the city, and entered the great plant of Strathdore and Son.

Opening the door of his own office, he passed through into that of his father, turned on the lights, and sat down. He looked at the desk, touched it here and there, dropping his hands upon his knees, absorbed in thought, how long he could not tell.

His mind raced back in a moment to a time when, as a small lad, he had seen his father place his hand somewhere on that desk. Suddenly a little hole opened. He had asked what it was? For answer the reply came that it was a "fairy hole," which contained a great secret that some day he might know.

"Strange!" thought Hal, as he continued to pass his hands over the desk in the region of what he could remember. "Strange!" he said aloud. "In my mind that panel seemed to move. I wonder if it was a real thing, or have I but dreamed it; children easily get such hallucinations. Perhaps it is only some fairy tale, or fable, mixed up with Aladdin and his wonderful lamp. Who knows?"

Once more before he left, he again passed his hands over the wood of the desk, pressing here and lifting there. He was about to give up the search for the night as hopeless when a click arrested him, and to his astonishment, the opening was revealed, just as he had seen it long ago.

Bending nearer, and bringing the light into position that he could see clearly, he looked inside. His heart bounded. Yes; there was the blue document, dust covered. Evidently for years it had not been touched, perhaps not since the day he had so innocently asked the question.

He perused it carefully, a smile of triumph playing over his face, followed by one of perplexity, then he turned his steps homeward, but not to sleep.

Hour after hour he strode up and down the carpeted room, occasionally stopping before the open window to gaze out upon the waters of the Gulf of Georgia where the moonbeams played in ripples of gold and silver across its surface.

If he could only see Nora, what a relief it would be to both. Would morning never come?

While Hal and Nora were deep in conversation the following day, as they ate their luncheon together, events were developing in the office of Burdette, Burdette, and Clarke.

"Good morning, Mr. Strathdore," said Burdette, as he rose to greet his client. "More legal business? You look troubled. These are hard times for the employers of labour. Nobody is satisfied with anything nowadays. This wretched war has upset everything; the world's agog."

"Oh, it is not that," said Strathdore, as he somewhat wearily took the proffered chair. "I only wish it were. It is another line altogether."

Explaining as rapidly as possible the cause of his only too apparent anxiety regarding Hal and Nora, he rambled on, "Young people are so different today from when I was young. Parents used to guide the on-coming generation in their choice of a future. Now they will not even listen; take things in their own hands, never even consider parents at all. But most assuredly Mr. Burdette, Hal cannot marry her now. It's against all moral and civil law. I cannot and will not give up what I've set my heart on these many years."

Burdette, touched by the intense earnestness of the man, said, "Send the boy to me, Mr. Strathdore, and let me see if I can persuade him to put things in their proper relative position."

"You will not, of course, make him aware of what I have told you Mr. Burdette? I feel we must keep that an utter secret if we are to succeed."

"Oh, no, no, leave that to me. I think I can handle the situation. Of a surety, there will be no difficulty with the girl. As a rule women are too conscientious to risk such a marriage, especially her type. Besides, if the worst comes to the worst, the fear of prison walls will no doubt fix that. I'll try Hal first — and failing, then we must work from the girl's side of the case. By the way, did you say that Miss Towers has a written declaration of her mother's just before death?"

"Yes, unearthed it from among some old papers after her aunt's death a short time ago. It was she who brought her to this Province. The other, she secured from the books in the office where she went to work after I dismissed her. It was quite by accident, but these two things make for absolute proof. You cannot get away from it. Never did I dream that it could be unearthed. It seems incredible. A belief in a retribution here and not in the hereafter is dawning on my soul."

Unheeding these remarks, for in his experience as a lawyer, Burdette had seen the [un]ravelling of too many "loose ends of the thread" of regrettable occurrences and sins to easily upset his equilibrium, so continued: "You say you are perfectly sure she has the proof, and your denial would be of no avail? Blackmail for instance?"

Strathdore nodded his head, while a shadow of intense agony crossed his handsome face. Though a man of over sixty years of age, he was an extremely well kept man of still striking appearance.

Burdette frowned, saying, "that's bad, but we will see what can be done. The case is not utterly hopeless. Get Hal to me as soon as you can, on some errand, and while here I shall sound him out, and find what he is thinking about in this regard. Then, as the door closed — "A deuce of a mess. Regular spider's web with the old chap inside I fear. Ah, well, the grist he has put into the mill has been slow in the grinding, but it is grinding."

The oblique rays of the sinking sun told of another day's work over. The office was quiet, save for the sounds which reached it from the thoroughfare below, as James Strathdore still sat in his easy chair musing.

The office fixtures, books, files and furniture, faded from his vision, and another obtruded. It was spring time, [in] an old fashioned garden, way down in the eastern part of Ontario. A handsome youth, in the flush of manhood, hurries to a picket gate, lifts the crude latch over which the lilacs hung their pink tipped cones; while beneath them, on a rustic seat, waited a sweet faced girl of some eighteen summers.

At the well known click [of the gate] and a low call [of her name], she springs to her feet to meet him. Once more he encircles her with his arm, and again tells her the sweetest of all stories, the memory of which brings a tear to his eye and trickles down his cheek.

A ring at the telephone brings him out of his dream. "Hello. No, not at the present time — busy. No, cannot see you tonight."

The next day found Hal seated in the office of Burdette and Co. When their business was completed, [Burdette] in a most casual way, began to talk of other matters.

"By the way, your father was here the other day, talking over private affairs. He has his heart set on your marrying Kathleen Tremaire, for some reason or other, which perhaps you know. Of course, it would make a strong firm, and I see no reason for you not at least considering the matter. He's dead set against this fancy of yours for Miss Towers. You gain nothing by such a marriage. Think before you act. As an old friend as well as a client, I would do anything I could to lift this cloud from his mind and heart. He's been awfully decent to you, Hal. Given you everything that you wanted. Besides you surely know that Miss Towers is not exactly in your class."

For a moment or two the younger man sat perfectly rigid, brows closely knit. [He] was about to rise and go, then apparently changing his intentions, burst forth with, "Oh, hang class! There may be some things that you ought to know before you try to force me into doing a thing which no man could do, and call himself a man." Putting his hand into his pocket, he drew forth a folded paper, handing it to the lawyer saying, "Read that." Burdette's lips set tightly, then as quickly relaxed. "But Hal, the purpose of this absolutely prohibits your marriage to Miss Towers. It's a serious matter to defy the laws of God and man."

Another paper was placed in the lawyer's hands. "Before you give any further advice, will you please read this? I infer you know nothing of it, or your words of a few moments ago would never have been uttered. You must remember I am a boy no longer. I cannot and will not be pitched about like a cork on the water any more. I am a determined man."

The lawyer's eyes followed the typed lines of the document. A look of amazement overspread his countenance.

"So this is the crux of the situation! May I ask where you got it? Does your father know you have this?"

"No, he does not, nor shall he," came bruskly from the set moan of the young man, "not until I choose to tell him — and more — I expect you as my lawyer, as well as his, to respect my confidence."

Quietness reigned supreme over the usually busy plant of Strathdore and Son. The whistle had blown and the weary men and girls had joined the long procession toward their varied homes, as Hal entered his father's office to put away some letters on the file.

"Sit down a moment Hal, I want to speak to you," said the older man; but he ignored his request and stood.

"Did you see Burdette today?"

"Yes, I did, Father."

"Well?"

"Well what?"

"I want to know what decision you have come to. Do you still intend to ruin your career by marrying Miss Towers? I have been observing you lately, and see no signs of your relinquishing your attentions to her."

"Yes, I do," was the instant reply.

"Then I must take steps to prevent it. Rest assured you shall never marry her. I will not have this disgrace brought upon my name. If you have talked with my lawyer, then I presume you know the worst. You would marry a girl without a name. My son never can nor shall. Tomorrow the machinery will be set in motion to sever forever your name from mine in this firm."

"There is no disgrace attached to the girl whatsoever. If what you suggest is true, and I presume it is, you say so. It surely is not her fault."

"I am sorry, Hal, that you take the attitude you do. [I am] indignant that you have so little gratitude for all I have done for you. Surely there is something coming to me, some consideration." He paused a moment, but Hal remained perfectly quiet.

"What I am about to do Hal, now, I had hoped never to be compelled to; but the emergency of the case demands that I enlighten you still further. Sit down."

"Thank you, I prefer to stand."

Turning to his desk, Strathdore senior pressed the panel, which had cost Hal so much trouble a few days before. It opened at his lightest touch. He bent forward, a look of consternation overspreading his usually composed face. Springing to his feet, he faced Hal, only to see in his hands the document of which he was in search.

"Stubborn and willful I know you are, but that I harboured a sneak, I never dreamed."

Hal clenched his fist, raised his hand, his face flaming; took one step forward, then remembering, he slowly let his hand fall by his side, while the crimson hue died from his face, leaving it ashen white.

"Father — and it may be the last time I shall ever call you by that name — years ago you opened that secret drawer, when I was but a tiny tot. I saw you put the blue paper inside the opening. My interest was seeing the panel slide. In answer to my childish question you said, 'There is a great secret in here that some day you may know.' To this day I have never in any way meddled with the drawer; but through the urge of recent circumstances I was forced to every and any avenue of escape from the tangle of life in which I am involved. It was you who put up the challenge in this game. I accepted it. There was naught else to do. I felt justified (when something urged me to see what that secret was) in any tactics that would help me to a just and right solution of the difficulty. 'All's fair in love or war,' the old adage runs. This was both. Are you satisfied with the result?"

"Give me that document. It is not yours, you scoundrel. You shall suffer for this."

Hal obeyed instantly saying, "It is of no use now as a secret, nor in legal procedure against me, when the facts are all known. It has been duly copied and witnessed; both Nora and I know that I am your adopted son, the son of an old friend who was killed in a mining disaster. His will left me to you, in case of anything befalling him, for I was utterly alone in the world. And now it is my turn to tell you a story. Let me touch the springs of memory, and tell you what you should have told me long ago if you knew who Nora was, when we were thrown unavoidably so much together. You thought her the finest secretary you ever had."

Strathdore listened in silence, no word escaped his [ears]. Hal stepped close to his side, his voice grew soft and low. A touch of tenderness for the man he had so long called father.

"Listen, Father — I know who Nora is — she is your own natural daughter. We are to be married in the vestry of the church, very quietly this evening. Will you come to the wedding? In gratitude for all you have done for me, and for my excellent upbringing, let me thank you. I appreciate it more than I can express in words. How sorry I am that thus ends the firm of Strathdore and Son, is beyond my ability to utter. Next month I shall take over the management of the Temaire interests, with a share in the Company. Mr. Temaire is growing too feeble to longer stand the strain. Till then we shall be in California; and more, Kathleen Temaire is to marry Lord Alvison in the autumn, when she returns from Europe, and live the life she most cares for, on the old English estate, bequeathed him by his forebears. He is now the Earl of K —."

Strathdore, shaken as by some mighty unseen force, sank into the chair, head bowed, and face covered with a trembling hand.

Once again he saw the old familiar scene — it was the old fashioned garden. The lilacs with their pink tipped cones had faded, and it was autumn. The maples had donned their brocaded mantles of russet and gold, as the figure of a man in life's full flush pauses a moment to gaze at the empty seat.

He does not lift the latch or give the accustomed call; then passes on a short distance down the road, enters the village cemetery, standing with uncovered head beside a newly made grave.[2]

The last rays of the sun have fled, while a meadow lark sings his evening song of praise to the god of day.

---

[2] This is the gravesite of Nora's deceased mother, with whom Strathdore Sr. had had an affair.

"NO TELLING WHAT MIGHT HAPPEN"[3]

The busy dock of the Canadian Pacific's Steamship Company at Vancouver was a mass of human beings. Seldom was it crowded to the extent of that June morning of 1898.

These were the days of the trek into the Klondike. Men of every description were there. Americans, Canadians, Norwegians, Swedes, as well as those from no country to which they held any allegiance, mongrels, drifters of fortune, from any and every land under the sun.

As one stood there on an elevated portion of the dock and watched the surging stream of humanity, if you were a keen observer, there were four men among the throng who would have attracted your attention. They were not together as four, and to the casual observer they were simply two in one spot, and two in another, busily lugging their effects on to the already heavily laden vessel. You would have noticed also that as the goods were placed on the deck, one of the men was always beside the rapidly increasing pile. They were dressed in ordinary business suits, somewhat the worse for wear.

If asked "whither bound?" the answer would have been, "The land of golden dreams, to stake our all on a venture there."

Each man as he ascended the gangplank carried, or more properly, dragged after him huge bundles, bags, valises and whatnot. They were bound for an unknown land, with very vague ideas of its ability to supply their wants. Hence the motley array of stuff which they piled for want of a better place) here and there on the decks of the boat. Soon the steamer was crowded to capacity, with every conceivable type of man, the long and the short, the fat and the lean. The man of education, mingled with the low born and ignorant from eastern lands. The man who ate his soup with signs of good breeding touched elbows with the one who took his with the sound of bathing in it.

It was surely a motley crowd, and Donald MacDonald, Harry Larchmont, Will Smith and Tom Harcourt were in striking contrast to most of those with whom their lot was cast.

The hold was crammed with all kinds of supplies. Everything was there, from pick axes to chewing gum, and overalls to tobacco. So when these men stood on the deck the great question was where to put all they had brought with them.

---

[3] Constance Lynd, "Came to Yukon Under Queer Conditions," *Calgary Herald*, December 22, 1923, p. 7.

The four men were crowded into one cabin, all they could possibly get. Every conceivable space was occupied with their immediate belongings, so with the four of them in the one small room, there was no place for their cargo. A hasty consultation took place, here and there, as they moved about the deck, two speaking a moment in one spot, and then passing to where one could apparently casually say a few words to another of the group. As Donald MacDonald emerged from the cabin the fourth or fifth time, he said to Tom Harcourt, who was standing beside their cargo, "Our stateroom is at the back, right in the centre of the aft-deck. There will be some protection from rain there, at least, so I guess we will just have to take the chances and pile it outside of our window; we can watch it there. All the fellows are having to do the same, every inch of room is taken. You ought to just see the trick it is to even get to one's berth. No use arguing, we've got to do it." Then, lifting his hand high above his head a moment (a signal that was quickly seen by Harry Larchmont, and passed on to Will Smith). These in turn came leisurely up to where Tom was standing, and in rotation loading up with the parcels went in various directions to the rear of the boat, depositing on the open deck their precious freight.

It consisted of parcels neatly done up, in rubber cases, perhaps 18 inches by 12 by 12. Here they piled all close to the stateroom wall under the window, in neat and compact form. Over it they then threw a heavy tarpaulin from among their supplies.

They were "going to Dawson to start in the stationery business," so they said, to inquiries as to the contents of the parcels.

When all was arranged, Larchmont and MacDonald stood by the rail, seemingly looking at the ceaseless stream of men passing up the gangway. Occasionally his eye would wander in the direction of their goods stacked on deck, and a troubled expression would flit over his usually placid countenance. In response to one of these, Larchmont said: "Look here, old boy, there is absolutely no use of worrying, what can't be cured, must be endured. It's up to us to watch out, that's all."

Finally, every man was on board. The last piece of baggage and freight had been safely landed. The gangplank was drawn up, the stern rope pulled up, as the engine began to throb and the vessel backed out from the dock into the open water. The shadows of night settled round them, while the stars peeped out, looking with silent wonder as they pursued their course.

The four men settled down to make the best of their surroundings. All save Smith retired for the night, while he lay smoking on the top of the pile beneath their window.

The men had been detailed on shifts of three hours each, one of whom was always on watch, day and night, though not in any way to be noticed. In fact, save in their own room, no conversation was carried on as a group.

Morning dawned, and with it the necessity of securing their places at the table. MacDonald, Larchmont and Harcourt were in the line near the door. Smith was leisurely smoking at the stern of the boat, apparently admiring the scenery. Suddenly MacDonald remembered his money belt. He had left it in the stateroom. How he hated to give up his perfectly good place in the line for breakfast — he was hungry. But the thought of what the loss of that belt might mean, sent him swiftly to secure it — if it were not already gone. No one was sure of anything, among this crowd. He opened the door, fearing to look at his berth. But there it lay, safely covered by his pyjamas — a belt containing some ten thousand dollars intact. He was perfectly well aware there would be easily a dozen who had they known, would gladly have relieved him of his burden.

Hastily slipping it on, he turned to the line, only to find the others had passed on — and the door shut.

Already another line had formed, so he sauntered out on deck, passed Smith with a casual "good morning," looked at the stuff, on top of which they had piled sacks of tools, axe, hammer and saws.

He was intently gazing at the pile when he was startled by —

"That your baggage?" said a voice from the Emerald Isle.

"What you got in there?" as he gave the bundles a kick. "Hard isn't it? Sure, ye've brought a lot of it."

"Stationery and supplies for a store we are going to open at Dawson," said MacDonald.

"Anything good to ate?" said he of the Irish brogue, "my stomach's wonderin' if my throat's been cut."

"No, nothing at all, unless you care to try digesting pens, paper, blotting pads and such like."

"Thank ye, no; but beyant you afeared it'll get wet afore you git thar?"

"Yes, rather. Though the cloth covering the bundles is rubber lined. We knew there was danger of not getting it in the hold so we prepared for it. I have some of the best in my room. But in any case the tarpaulin should keep it all right."

"Four ave ye, going to keep store." This said as half question and half exclamation. But it gave MacDonald as queer feeling as the man, a stranger looked at him with a strange sidelong glance, then said, "Ye must be 'specting to be busy."

The words, with the accompanying look, startled him. How did he know there were four — was the secret out? With never the slightest change of expression, he replied, "No, no, two of the men you have seen me with are friends, and the other and myself will run the store. The other two are out for gold. It is our venture. Dawson is going to be a great place and we are taking a chance to get in on the ground floor. We have found that it is almost impossible to get supplies of this kind, even to write letters — then too, we are carrying some reading matter, magazines and books too."

He drew his under lip firmly up under his long determined upper lip with a "Humph! Wall, guess I'll go and try and git some grub. Naw books for me today." So saying he shuffled off leaving MacDonald to his thoughts. Seeing the other two approaching, he touched Smith on the arm saying, "Come on Smith and let us see if we can get something to eat."

Larchmont and Harcourt sauntered along the deck, seating themselves on the tarpaulin, smoking and talking, evidently in utter abandon.

A heavy fog permeated the air — soon it lifted, revealing a scene of unusual beauty. Everyone was at the deck's rail, gazing on the wonderful scenery. Later on in the day, some were drinking, some sleeping or some smoking, while others wanted occupation and were eagerly seeking places to play cards.

There was hurrying and scurrying to find any available thing that could be construed into a table.

"I say, Scotty," for MacDonald wore a Scotch cap, "what you say to letting us have some packages of yere blessed note paper? It would make foine tables and sates too."

"All right," was the reply, "providing there is no drinking near it, to spoil it. Do you hear?"

Willing hands got to work, to erect the table. Bundle after bundle was placed until the right height was attained, and others were ended up for seats.

"Come along, Scotty, and take a hand, and yese can watch yere blomin paper at the same time."

With a grim smile, MacDonald seated himself beside a rough appearing man, of foreign extraction, yet who spoke English perfectly. The game proceeded — some money changed hands — not much though, until the dinner hour arriving put an end to the game.

The men restored the packages to their place on the deck, covering them carefully with the tarpaulin. This was a wise precaution to insist on, for day after day the men used the packages for tables and chairs, when the weather was fine, and as MacDonald always saw that a certain formation was carried out in placing them, he could tell at a glance if any were missing.

The days passed in quick succession as they wound their course in and out among the Islands. Such beauty of scenery. Wonderful colouring of the islands, decked out in all the glory of the first wild flowers on the one side, and the mainland on the other. It was a constant panorama. Here and there a glacier dipped its icy surface to the very edge of the water, seeming to shimmer in the sunlight as shadow and shade played across its bosom.

Some days everyone was cross and cranky on the steamer, owing to the confinement on the over-crowded vessel. Everyone was ready to fight, and they did, but, if you were a careful observer you would have found one or the other of these men either stretched out on the tarpaulin, or sitting somewhere nearby, indifferently smoking. They were really days of anxiety to the men. They never knew what turn affairs might take, and in some sort of a mix-up with the men, might find their goods all overboard.

But on, ever on, past Queen Charlotte's Islands, past Juneau, with its wonderful colouring of grass and spring flowers, until at last the company were freed from their seemingly long confinement, as the steamer drew up alongside the dock at Skagway.

Now began the most difficult part of their voyage. All hands were at work, transferring baggage, supplies of all sorts, to the cars of the Narrow Gauge railway, which had been built to carry men and freight over the once deadly White Horse Pass.[4] Here, where thousands of lives were sacrificed to the all-absorbing passion for gold. This road had been built to provide a means of carrying, to the head of navigation. Some hours later found our men depositing their cargo on the shores of Lake Bennett, while each

---

[4] Construction of the White Pass and Yukon Route Railway took twenty-six months, commencing in 1898 with completion in 1900. It was acknowledged to be a great engineering feat. From the base of the Pass to the summit, the railway climbs 962 meters in only 38 kilometers of track. It was built from the seaport of Skagway, Alaska, to transport prospectors and supplies to the headwaters of the Yukon River where they would then go by boat to the goldfields around Dawson City. Before the railroad was constructed, prospectors travelled on foot over the treacherous Chilkoot Pass to gain access to the headwaters.

was ready to do his part in the construction of some craft to take them down the stream to their destination.

So far everything had gone as well as they could have expected. This was the trying part of the journey. Fear haunted them lest any word had leaked out of their real mission. Every precaution had been taken on the start. Each man arriving on a different train, and from different points.

It was one thing to sit tight on a steamer, snug and comfortable, and quite another to get their cargo off in the wilderness, with little or no facilities [for] taking care of it.

Axes, hammers and saws were then called into requisition, as those with larger amounts of freight set to work to build flat-bottomed scows on which they and their belongings would hope to float safely down the water-way even if there were some dangerous spots, while others, who carried their all in a pack, preferred to trudge on along the shores of the rivers and lakes to their destination — Dawson.

Some built simply rafts, and sometimes they made the journey safely, often not. But for so prepossessing a looking craft as these men were planning to build, to be caulked and varnished with ship varnish on the outside, there were many offers of assistance, free of charge, save the opportunity to get a ride downstream and save the long tramp by land.

The four men, though apparently totally absorbed in their shipbuilding, were very watchful of the men they gave the chance of the ride with them. Once launched on the unknown waters, except as they had received written instructions of their peculiarities, there was no telling what might happen. There might be among the passengers of the steamer those who were just waiting for this very opportunity. The whole of these might be overpowered and pitched into the river — yet they did really need three other men at least. Days and days of a journey on an unknown river lay before them — they must work in relays. As for themselves, things had to be so arranged that day and night someone fresh and not inclined to sleep should be on duty as guard. MacDonald chose as one of the crew his friend of the Emerald Isle. He had watched him closely and his Scotch head told him he was safe.

They were quite safe, at the head of navigation, as scores of others were engaged in the same building operations as these four.

Everything was now ready, the last bundle safely piled in the scow. MacDonald had given the others orders to have their automatics loaded fully — to take no chances. Each man was now, they felt, his own policeman, his own law.

They were anxious days, yet not without their full quota of enjoyment. It did not take long to discover there were breakers ahead, for here and there they would come across the wreckage of some similar craft, or raft that had capsized and lodged on the rocks, often much too near the surface of the water. The numerous rapids tested all their skill of seamanship to prevent accident.

Night was the most trying time. There was no possibility of doing anything else but to tie up as the shadows of evening fell; though days were long, yet they must have rest. Two slept on board, while the others rolled in their blankets, slept the sleep of the just, lulled to rest by the sound of the rippling water, while the moon and stars kept watch above.

Lake Bennett and Lake Tagish were safely passed and they were now traversing the waters of the Lewis River, on which were very treacherous rapids, before the entering of the Yukon River. At last they were on the last lap of their journey. Twenty-four hours before they reached Dawson they saw someone waving frantically to them from the shore. Harcourt took his binoculars from his satchel to make sure of what sort of a party was awaiting them. To the great joy of all it was Henry St. John, who had gone out the autumn before, to prepare for this very event.

They soon pulled alongside and took him on board. What a feeling of relief to have someone thoroughly acquainted with the country.

The next day Dawson was sighted and ere the evening shadows (for they were only shadows) had fallen, the scow had been fastened to a tree by the water's edge, and the five men unloaded its contents onto an improvised sled which St. John had ready for the transferring of their property to safe keeping.

As soon as they docked, the other men had jumped and fled. One thought alone filled their minds — grub and a bed, for the provisions had run short and they had been on limited rations for the past two days.

The five men came down the main street of the then embryo city, two pulling the sled through the slippery mud, for a drizzling rain was falling, while the others had their arms full of such as would not accommodate itself on the sled.

They stopped in front of a wooden shake-like building over the door of which was a sign — hand printed — on a long streamer of cotton:

BOOKS This Store will be opened
for One Hour on Thursday
from
Four P.M. to Five P.M.

Inside with their freight, the doors were securely bolted — a meal was soon served. Never did food taste better than to these tired, weary men, at last relieved from the tension of their long voyage.

Then for the first time all four men lay down to sleep, with never a care or worry, leaving a husky dog and a policeman from a near-by barracks to keep watch. Morning saw them at work, with hammers, nails and screws, preparing for the event of the afternoon. Counters had been erected by the industry of St. John, while the others divided them off into sections, erecting two cages, well wired in.

Before four o'clock, the hour for the opening of the store, quite a crowd had gathered, eager to see anything new to add excitement to their isolated lives. Simultaneously, the blinds were lifted, the door unlocked — and by the pull of a rope the sign was reversed, to reveal to the expectant men, and a few women, the following:

Dawson's First Bank

———————

Bank of British North America
Capitalized at $1,500,000[5]

———————

N.B. - Gold dust weighed and
taken in exchange for money

The stationery had become bills of all denominations, marked with a stamp of red and yellow, and Dawson printed across the face. Without this, the bills were of no value.

This was done in case of a robbery so they could be easily traced.

Beneath the floor of the bank St. John had (often while others slept) excavated an opening that served for a vault.

So, without safe protection, or a strong box, $1,500,000 had been carried on the deck of a steamer openly, and deposited in the first bank of Dawson City.

What a relief to find that each night they might sleep in safety. For beside them slept a North West Mounted Policeman, and out-

———————

[5] There is a discrepancy in Emily's text. She typed both $15,000,000 and $1,500,000.

side could be heard all the night through, the steady footfall of the city police, watching with trusty eye and ear that no harm should come to so valued an institution.

At this time there were some one hundred and fifty Mounted Police in the country. It's no wonder we had law and order there. These men have been the very foundation of country's peace and safety.

"THE BROWN THRUSH"[6]

It was a beautiful June morning such as only the West can produce, when Lucy McMillan alighted from the train at Lethbridge, the end of steel in the early eighties.

Young, bright and cheerful, added to these qualities was a vivaciousness she has never lost, though much that she has passed through in the intervening days would have worn out a weaker spirit.

She had not the honour of "coming up in a Red River cart," but she did have the honour of coming farther west to her destination in Alberta by the first stage coach from Lethbridge to Macleod.

She had reached Medicine Hat on the main line of the Canadian Pacific Railway (then a very primitive line), in the days when a train might be delayed for an indefinite time owing to a huge herd of wild cattle crossing the tracks. Nothing stopped them, and even the powerful CPR was compelled to stand at attention when those giants of the prairie passed by. The road from this point to Lethbridge was a little old narrow gauge, known more familiarly as a "turkey trail," really a coal road into the Galt coal mines.

As she stepped from the train that early June morning, and saw the stage coach standing ready to carry the passengers who arrived further west, her first words were to the driver, "Man, be sure you get us home before midnight, or like Cinderella, we may be turned into a pumpkin."

"No, sir-ee! madam!" was the reply, "this here stage coach won't turn into no pumpkin, it is the real stuff." Then, having carefully stowed all the passengers and baggage away inside and on top, he mounted the seat, black snake whip in hand, feeling very much his position as the one and only connecting link between primitive and modern transportation.

---

[6] Constance Lynd, "Knew the Old Time West in the Rough and Ready Days when Pollinger and his Coach Provided the Transportation," *Calgary Herald*, May 10, 1924, p. 8.

Were it not for Pollinger, how could these people ever cross the miles of waste? Pollinger and his coach were to the railroad and old Fort Macleod what the coupling was to the car and engine. In fact, so much importance did he attach to his position that the West could never have been — but for Pollinger.

As Lucy McMillan took her seat in the coach that summer morning, mingled feelings surged over her, and in quick succession there passed before her mental vision the friends she had left in the East. Her father (the old squire) and mother and all the family — she could see them all, and the old home. How delightful it looked from this far away view. The large old rambling house, vine covered, with here and there a rambler rose peeping out with its eyes of red, yellow or pink, from among the greenery. The old orchards and beyond the vineyards. She saw again the maples, and elms bending low, their branches, and somehow a choking sensation crept over her as she looked around for some familiar trees. But none were to be seen, only the bald bare prairie. How could she know that the trees that did exist were lying low in the bottoms of the coulees. And then they were not her trees, but the poplar and the balm of Gilead, or as more commonly known, the cottonwood.

She thought of the tremendous distance she had travelled, and the impossibility of her return, when suddenly youth, with its constant vision of the future, loomed before her eyes, and instead of the loved ones she had left behind there appeared another face — the face of a young man, brown haired and brown eyed, James Nichol, whose bride she was to be as soon as the stage coach pulled into Macleod.

The day after the wedding the presents began to pour into their home, which was the usual shack of three rooms, already prepared for her. Her husband was the manager of Senator McFarren's lumber business, the first in this part of the country. Among the presents were dishes — "barrels of them" — chairs, piano lamps, albums "a yard long," and last but not least, two calves already branded with L. N. From these she, in the years that followed, became the proud possessor of quite a herd. All save the calves had been shipped from Winnipeg for the coming bride. It was a real western welcome.

Macleod was one of the old forts where dwelt the "Riders of the Plains," our noble North West Mounted Police to whom we owe the safety, order and peace of the West.

Here dwelt Col. Steele and wife, Col. and Mrs. Sanders (now police magistrate of Calgary) and their wonderful detachment of "men of iron," with hearts of tenderness, to the number of about two hundred. These, with the Hudson's Bay factor John Black and staff, made up the bulk of the citizens of the little town of Macleod.

John Black played a great part in reaching the hearts of the Indians, while Cols. Steele and Sanders were the centre of the social world of the place. Too much cannot be said of the part they played in the early development of the country.

There were three little churches, Presbyterian, Methodist and Catholic. These were the days of the freighters, caravans, and no bridges to cross the mountain streams made treacherous by the rapidly melting snows of the mountains.

Some weeks later, when the young couple had become settled, the town was all astir early. It was the day of the annual picnic at Bovis lake, a beautiful spot up in the mountains.

It was the usual custom to initiate all the newcomers, or, as they were called, "tenderfeet," to the mysteries of the West.

Such a bustling — riders and drivers, all the old timers and their families. The older ones drove in the four-horse wagons, while the youngsters rode any and all sorts of ponies and horses, even to the old Indian cayuse. The two hours of driving saw them at the spot where the day's festivities were to take place, for it was to be a great day.

Shortly after the numerous baskets, kettles, boxes, pails, and not to forget the bottles, etc., had been safely stowed away out of the reach of the hot July sun, two of the old-timers, Mr. Willock and Mr. Kettles (whose children are still in the district), went up to the young bride and, taking her by the arm on either side, said, "This is the day of your initiation. Come."

They led her, clothes and all, knee deep into the water. Taking a handful of water they put it on her head, christening her the "Brown Thrush" — partly because of her voice, which they had heard in song, ever since she had arrived, and the piano [was] installed in their home.

"Weren't you wet?" I asked. "Yes, but later on Judge Ives' father took pity on me and drove me to their nearby home where I got dried."

Some two weeks later, she and her husband rode into the mountains to look over the lumber camps and also to see if any fires were kindling. Fires have lost to Canada millions of feet of timber that a little care and thought might have saved.

"Such a revelation!" I shall quote her own words: "I shall never forget it. Leaving our horses part way up, we ascended to the top.

Clouds beneath, a double rainbow in the distance. For the first time I looked from that tremendous height over primitive nature. Away below lay the city of the tents of the lumbermen. I stood spellbound, wishing that I had all the infidels in the world there to see — they'd go down with a firm faith in a great Creative Being, whom we call God."

There come great moments in life when we stand face to face with God in his works of nature. These were some of such.

A week later, the two, Mr. and Mrs. Nichol, started to a drive of some distance over the prairies. As they bumped along in the not too springy democrat, suddenly the tongue broke. Releasing one of the horses, Mr. Nichol prepared for a fifteen mile ride to get help or something to mend the broken rig.

The horses were too wild to allow of her accompanying him, and more than that, it was to be a bare back ride, so there was nothing for her to do, but to sit still and wait for his return. These were not the days of motor cars and a garage at every crossroads. In fact, there were no crossroads as yet, only the occasional meeting of the Indian trails.

"Alone in the desert" were the words that came to her mind as she saw her husband disappear over the horizon. Not a tree, not a human being or dwelling in sight. Suddenly, she perceived mere specks moving in all directions. Nearer and nearer they came. As far as the eye could reach the prairie appeared to be moving.

A closer view revealed the fact that they were Indians. Men and women, old and young, horses, dogs, travois and papooses gathered round her.

She was startled, but there was nothing to do but sit there come what would. The moment that anything was seen on the prairie those days, as if by magic they came. No sound of human voice gave the alarm. It was their reserve, their land, and they must see what it was. As they gathered around her she felt her last hour had come. How good the old home near Montreal looked then. Would her husband never come?

Closer and closer they came, till they had closed in round the wagon. Her hat had been lost in the wind and her hair was flowing down her back. The old chief touched her, then seeing that she was frightened, he began to stroke her hair, saying "Expisuya," as he strung his fingers through the light hair. Continuing his stroking of the hair, he said "Expisuya" meaning "White Squaw" — then laughed, which was instantly followed by a burst of laughter from the assembled crowd.

At this juncture she saw a rider come into sight. It was [a] friend of [hers] and never did human being look so good as he. He sprang from the horse and proceeded to repair the break.

Instantly the Indians began to move, and a few minutes later not a being was in sight. They had all disappeared into the bottoms or coulees where were their tepees.

Oh, yes, the Masons were here in those days; perhaps the gathering was more of a social club than the carrying out of the real principles of Masonry. However, you shall judge for yourselves. Any Mason can tell you whether this is real Masonry.

There had been a series of these banquets — and there were also ten newly arrived brides in the town. These ten brides were left at home alone until the "wee small hours of the morning," while their men "rode the proverbial goat."[7]

Naturally they felt neglected. Had they not come out to this country with all their new clothes, with little or no chance to show them? They laid a plot. The real reason of the plot was the condition of their husbands from being butted by said "goat"on their return from said banquets.

It was the midnight hour when the ten sallied forth. They reached the hall, tapped gently on the door. To their amusement the keeper of the door flung it wide open, saying in a maudlin voice, "Merry Christmas," when it was only March.

The voices of the fair young brides had an electrical effect. One swift movement and every man ducked head first under the table saying as he went, "It's the girls!" Under the table they went heads first and legs sprawling out behind. So funny was the sight of these men, at least the legs sprawling out behind, that the girls were all convulsed with laughter. One [man] was heard to remark, "Well man was kin to the ostrich." One: it is the first time I ever knew that man alone stood his ground and faced the attacking force. As his amazement cooled and he got breath to speak, he said, "Men, it's all up, they've got us buffaloed."

It was the last of the banquet nights; forever after they had Masonic "At Homes," and husbands and wives together enjoyed the evening — and the men went home sober.

Does anyone undervalue the service the CPR has rendered this country in building their wonderful transcontinental road? Building it when there was nothing much here, save Indians, buffaloes, cattle, deer, coyotes and gophers.

---

[7] This is an adage used to describe a drinking party.

Perhaps few knew of the difficulties that beset them in their work. As fast as they mapped out the roadway, the Indians followed stealthily, pulling the pegs and flags up as rapidly as they could put them in.

With the coming of the railroad and all its branches, the old passed out. The freighter, the string team, prairie schooner, and the cowboy were gradually obliterated, while civilization came, and a new era dawned. In fact, transportation is the basis of all development.

To Mr. and Mrs. Nichol were born five children. The very best kind of immigration for Canada's vast spaces.

After living at Pincher Creek for a number of years, the family came to Calgary fifteen years ago for the sake of the education of the children.

Mrs. Nichol has ever been a devoted church member, singing in the choir till the present time. During the war as she went about the country, especially in the mining camps and outlying districts, she brought many hundreds of dollars to the Red Cross. All through those dreadful years, with her three boys at the front, she worked untiringly at the Red Cross depot. Two of her children are university graduates, the other three are all fine Canadian citizens and occupy good positions.

Hardship and the lack of modern equipment did not leave her weak and helpless, and the years of toil have not made her old, but have developed in her the qualities of true womanhood. She is young today in spite of a few stray grey hairs and trips about "as sprightly as a girl," while as the "Brown Thrush," a name that has long since died away, she still sings her songs of thankfulness to the Heavenly Father, for the chance of having a part in the making of this great Western Canada.

She visits regularly the hospitals and anywhere that she can bring comfort to the sick ones. And, in our great Dominion sanatorium for tuberculosis, you will find her a regular visitor, bringing cheer and hope to those afflicted ones, many of whom are returned men.

Such were the women who, with the brave men, have ever been in the forefront as makers of Canada.

A CAUTIONARY TALE[8]

The day was warm and balmy, not a cloud in the sky; but there were in our hearts, dark, ragged, wind-torn clouds which we could not see a trace of dispelling. As we sat by the lake, having eaten our supper on the shore, we still lingered, until the last rays of the setting sun had gilded the hilltops; then Jack rose, saying in a most determined voice, "It's got to be, that is all there is to it, I will not stand for any more such nonsense. Why everyone who knows anything, and has any brains, is agreed, it is the right thing, even if it is new! These old folks who are so tied to custom and habit, ought to get off this globe and leave it to youth. That is what I say."

I was a girl of some seventeen summers, and the boy (for such I call him now) was nineteen, who had delivered himself of the forgoing ideas. I swallowed it all deeming him a Solomon for his display of wisdom, especially as it fitted exactly into my scheme of things. His name was Jack Shaffer, mine Nell Adaire; and both of us in high school.

Secretly I had begun to read Judge Ben Lindsey's ideas in *Companionate Marriage*, thinking little about it until I met the new boy from the big city of X — who had come to live near us.[9] The more I saw of Jack, and the more he talked of companionate marriage, the more was I convinced it was the only thing to stem the spectacle of many unhappy marriages, which the papers said, were made. I was certain that no one could or would know the right of things as did Judge Ben Lindsey.

Of course, it was a new idea, and one which my elders appeared very much against, so of course, it pleased me all the more;

---

[8] PAA, UCCA-AC Acc. No. 75.387, Box 181, Item 6027, Nell Adaire, "My Experience With Companionate Marriage," c. 1927. On the manuscript there is the typewritten name and address of Mrs. G. W. Kerby, 1125, 7th Avenue West, Calgary, Alberta, Canada.

[9] Benjamin Barr Lindsey (1869-1943) was an American judge and reformer. In 1927, together with Wainright Evans, Lindsey co-authored *Companionate Marriage* in which he advocated cohabitation before marriage, along with birth control, and no-fault divorce. This was a controversial work which drew widespread criticism from many groups, including the church. Emily did not criticize Lindsey for his views on birth control, and she remained silent regarding divorce laws. Her attack on his ideas focused on common law relationships. Other social activists, including Judge Emily Murphy — Janey Canuck — also attacked cohabitation outside of marriage because of the harm they felt it exerted upon the family bond.

for I was fully convinced that the wisdom of the world centred in Jack.

I was not old enough to think matters through for myself, or to realize how ancient the marriage custom was, nor yet did I know how indelibly it was written in the human soul. It had to be for the sake of the child.

I knew that my father and mother did not always agree, and mistook their differences for unhappiness, which, had I been older, I would have known that any two people would at times disagree, and no harm be done. Mother was better educated than father; he was a businessman who had worked himself up to a place of prominence. I felt that some day I would marry, and was perfectly confident that I could make a better try at the job than they had. In fact, I really desired to marry when the time came.

With all these ideas, and having devoured Judge Ben Lindsey, the stage was all set for results when the new boy came to the city. It was all so easy, and if one husband did not suit, why I could try again until he did suit me in every way, a rather large contract for human beings to undertake.

Having fully decided that our parents were very old fashioned, so crazy were we to try this new thing of which everyone was talking, some in favour, but far more against; but of course we knew these people were so ignorant. We talked of what fun it would be to be married and go on to school; how envious others would be of us; what a joy to do our lessons together in the evenings; it all had such a halo over it, we could not resist and be happy.

We decided that each should attack their parents on the subject at once, which we did, but with utter consternation on each side was our request received.

Growing restless under their prohibition, we planned the next move, which was this: I declared to mine that if they did not consent, I was going to drown myself, and Jack affirmed his decision of starting for Timbuchtoo [sic] or some other outlandish place if there was not consent given on the side of his progenitors.

Oh! how bejoyed we were, to think we had won out — the new over the old. Yes, they were really back numbers, as were all who disagreed with us. Our parents would not consent to our going on to school, but they would provide a small suitable house, each parents paying half, and Jack must get to work, and we were required to support ourselves.

We were the happiest pair alive as we took up our abode in our tiny home. For some three or four months all went well, and although parents did not approve, they did not interfere at all, and gave us every chance to be, and do, what we were so sure we could do, in building the ideal home.

As I said, for some months all went well, then came the rub. Jack had an office position with one of the railways — a good one too that paid well. The phone would ring about five o'clock, "Nell, my dear old thing! I will not come way up for dinner as I have to work tonight from seven to ten."

Of course, I would in the sweetest tones tell him of how lonely I would be and how long the evening would be until his return.

At first it was one night a week, which time I would spend at my mother's or with some of my girlfriends, but gradually the hour of return became later and later, and then from one night a week it became three and often four.

One evening I was at Mother's awaiting my husband as usual with the latent fear irking at my heart, when Mother said to me, "Nell, what is the matter with you? You are not yourself, nor have been for some time. I've noticed it, so has Mrs. Shaffer." Nervously wrought up as I was, and the fact that I was only yet a mere child, I broke down utterly, crying my heart out on my mother's knee, as I told her in plaintive words of what was going on, and how I wished I had listened to her.

Mother did not chide me. She knew I was bitterly hurt, and getting my own punishment for my youthful persistence. While she talked so quietly, she planned a clever *coup d'etat*, to trap my recalcitrant leige and lord, and find out the real meaning of his working so late, for now it was often the hour of two and three in the morning before he would arrive — but always with some perfectly plausible reason.

So, without the slightest doubt, we discovered that he had never been asked to work overtime at all. You may draw your own conclusions as to where the companionate husband of mine was.

A few evenings later, rising from the dinner table, he said, "Nell, I am so sorry, but I have to go again tonight to that beastly station at nine, and shall not be able to get in until nearly five." Then, lauding my patience to "put up so patiently" with his awful hours; what a darling I was, how he loved me for the fact I never scolded about it — so different from some girls. He was really sorry, but then, if we wanted to live, he must work.

That evening as soon as he had left, my father and mother came over to the house, and we packed up everything they had contributed to it, what was to be our ideal home, and moved them to their residence.

From that day to this, I have never seen Jack. I left no letter to explain, and he dared not go to my home, for I think my father would have horsewhipped him or shot him. So, thought I: thus ends "Companionate Marriage," a myth and a snare to trap foolish girls like me. Yes, fools. We were too young to know the real meaning of marriage.

The worst of it was, that like the little birds which have broken from the nest sooner than they should, I was not happy in my old home. I felt that people who had frowned on our adventure were gratified at the result, while others pitied. A month was the extent of my sojourn there, while I was seeking to get into something at which I could earn my living.

Having so hurt my parents, I could not but feel it would be kinder to them to go out again and make good.

Fortunately I had an aunt in the city of C — ; while visiting her I met one of the doctors of a large medical clinic, and through their influence, I got a position with them. There I worked my way from one post to another, for I was quick and not afraid of work; until I became quite an expert in the X-ray room.

Here I met Dr. Cardross, a man some eight years my senior. A junior in the firm, I was thrown with him constantly in his work and, although I admired him exceedingly, it never entered into my thoughts such a thing as ever again entering into matrimony. That was done for me. That line was a blank so far as I was concerned. I seemed perfectly indifferent to the opposite sex. He would drive me home at the evening sometimes, occasionally take me out somewhere, all in the same friendly way, so that when one evening we were coming home from a late piece of work in the clinic, I was utterly surprised when he told me how much he thought of me, and his desire to make me his wife.

Never was a human being taken more by surprise, for somehow I had a feeling as if the mark of Cain was upon me and that everyone read in my face my punishment for defying the laws of both man and God.

I could not answer him. I begged for time.

"Is there anyone else, Nell?

Don't you care for me at all?"

"Yes, I do, but it has all come as a rift in the sky, and before I can promise I must have time." So the days slipped. Sometimes I would decide that I would accept him, and try again; for I soon realized how very fond I was of him. Then would come a grave fear — if he should ever find out what I had done in the past, would he ever forgive my being such a fool? To tell him, I could not. I was so ashamed of my youthful folly that it was difficult for me to see in the Nell of today the impulsive determined girl of a few years ago.

At last I decided to take the chance, and as neither of us had families near, we were married quietly one evening, and on our return, Dr. Cardross took me to the loveliest home one could desire.

We made fine friends, we liked the same books, our interests coincided, and I was the happiest creature alive, especially after being sure that peace and joy could never be mine as the result of early folly. We were real companions.

Then when our first baby was expected, our cup of joy was more than full. When it was all over and I was about again, and the nurse gone, imagine my despair when my husband told me that our little son would be a helpless cripple, and would in all probability be blind later as well.

My husband did everything he could to try and make life less dreary for me, for I was obsessed with misery over it all. But I could not forget, nor could I banish it from my mind, one single moment of the waking hours; and so the days dragged on in fearful agony of mind and heart — my baby — my baby!

When about three months old he would look up into my face with such a pathetic gaze, it added new woe to my already burdened soul. I felt as though my heart must break. Did I love him? Yes! I loved him dearly, this little piece of mankind, he was ours; that was sufficient, and the agony of it all only added bitterness to my overwrought mind. A shadow seemed to envelop me, from which I could not extricate myself. Dread followed me day and night, yet I seemed not to know [why].

One evening, dinner had waited a long time for my husband's return, when the telephone rang saying, "I've been delayed and will not be back for half an hour. I'm at the General Hospital — a motor accident — young man dreadfully injured."

The next day after his visit to the hospital, my husband said while at luncheon, "By the way, that young man I find is from the same city as you; went to school with you. I happened to say that my wife was also from there — perhaps you might know each other."

For a moment my heart stopped beating, as, controlling myself, I asked his name.

"Jack Shaffer. He seems to have been all over the world, but one thing, he will never travel much farther — he's rotten clean through. Did you know much about him? When I told him who you were there was such a strange look came into his eyes, and then a sardonic smile quickly passed over his face. I did not know what to make of it — but he's rotten, rotten. Oh! That such creatures are left to live and inflict their diseases on the innocent."

I felt as if I turned to stone, but inwardly resolved to gain entrance to that hospital room and beseech him who had so spoiled my young life, not to divulge what he knew, though I had little hope he would grant my request.

But fate had other plans, and ere I could reach the hospital, being detained by circumstance — the damage had been done.

When my husband returned that evening there was none of his usual gaiety, and discussion of the day's events; but in place an ominous silence prevailed. The ghastly meal ended; he rose, requesting me to come into the study as he wanted to have a talk with me.

Such a look of pain I had not seen on my husband's face in my memory, as he stood, not even asking me to sit down. He burst forth, "Nell! Nell! It's not true. Tell me it's not true. I cannot believe it, unless you say so, I cannot."

"Believe what Gerald? What do you mean?" I barely whispered; my vocal cords refused to respond. "What is wrong, Gerald? Do tell me "

Deep furrows lined my husband's face, as in anguish he brokenly exclaimed, "Oh! Nell, that rotten fellow told me — he told me this morning when I went in to see him that at seventeen years of age, you were his companionate wife, and that you lived together for about a year." Then, placing his hands on my shoulder, he said, "Nell, Nell! Say it is not true. Say it. I cannot believe it."

"Yes, Gerald it is all true. I was young: Judge Lindsey had advocated it and Jack urged me, so I thought he knew what was best. I would not listen to either my father or mother. Our parents objected but we overruled them by threatening a more dire calamity."

I felt as if I had turned to stone; my voice seemed like the voice from a cavern, as I sank into a chair utterly exhausted.

The baby, our baby, was lying on the couch. Gerald gazed at the child for a moment, with love, pathos, and anger all mingled. Then pointing at it said, "Oh, Nell! Now I know what caused that little afflicted one — that rotten fellow. He must have infected you."

"Before I married you I was tested for a clean bill of health. I wanted to be sure. It did not occur to me to ask the same of you. I had such confidence in you. Why didn't you tell me? Why? It might all have been prevented."

Then, gathering up his instruments, [he] went up to his room, finally came down saying, "I've packed up my things. You may stay here with the child. I'll make an allowance for you in the meantime. A taxi will call for my trunks." He paused a moment on the threshold of the house — then passed out into the night.

The baby cried. I picked him up to nurse and quiet him, then laid him down. Immediately he went into the most dreadful convulsion I had ever seen, and before help arrived, the little life which had begun so marred and handicapped, passed out into the world of light — and I was alone with my dead.

A WESTERN WELCOME[10]

"Mother! is there a Jule-Missen in this country?[11] We had one in Iceland — does he ever come here to little boys and girls?" "Really, dear, I cannot say. It is my first Christmas here, you know, but I surely hope he does come to us." This was said to tide over the ache which was already gripping her own heart, the fear that Christmas would find them without the means of procuring what she would like to make the day a happy one, such as they had known in their native land.

"If there is no Jule-Missen here, I'm not going to stay," said the lad, as his face puckered in the attempt to keep back the tears which were dangerously near the surface.

"I won't either," came from the little sister Ingrid, in their own tongue.

The long summer days had passed swiftly away, and the lingering twilight of our western plains was fast receding from its reign of the past months. The first frost betokened the approach of winter. To Emil came thoughts of another land — far away. A great longing filled his heart, as, with blue eyes lifted to his mother's face, he asked wistfully, while he caught her skirt in an effort to detain her long enough to get an answer to the question which was uppermost in his mind. He had vivid remembrances of the

---

[10] Constance Lynd, "Emil's First Christmas in Canada," *Onward*, December 21, 1929, p. 403.

[11] This character is similar to the North American Santa Claus.

festal day so dear to childhood in his own land; he knew that Jule-Missen did come there.

When the first snow fell, his mind wandered to the old saying that some fairy "was picking her ducks for Christmas." His heart bounded with joy; then sank in the depth of despair. "What if this country were different, and there was no one to think of the little children?"

Again and again he asked the same question as the day approached, "Mother! will Jule-Missen come to us here in Canada?"

Sometimes he would sit very still a long time, a far-away look in his eyes, which always brought a shade of anxiety to his mother's bright, happy face. "What is the matter, my son? What are you thinking of so seriously?"

"Oh! Nothing; only how the fiords would now be all frozen over; the boys skating and skiing. I can see them sledding down the hills. I wish I had a sled."

Here was only prairie land, no streams or frozen lakes where he could go with other boys for his winter fun. Still, he was sure, he could get a pretty good ride (if only he had a sled) down the side of the hill into the coulee, where the barn had been erected for shelter. The country, too, seemed so big; he was afraid that Jule-Missen would never find them in this great land. And what if he did not understand English? One night in his old home he was lying awake on Christmas Eve, and had heard him speak — and he spoke the Icelandic language!

The child's parents were simple peasant folk; they had never possessed much of this world's goods, yet they had always been able to provide a real Christmas for their children. The day prior to the great event they all had their usual bath — sometimes the only one for the whole year. The shoes of the family had been placed at night in a row, side by side, to indicate that the family meant to live the coming year in peace. Very early the next morning, while still dark, they had risen to drive several miles to the church, through the frosty atmosphere, to celebrate the coming of the Christ. He had been born in the night; and so they had come to bow down before the image of the infant in the manger, as symbolized before them. Then to their homes where the day was spent in quiet peacefulness. This was their first year in Canada. Early in March they had crossed the Atlantic, then journeyed miles and miles without end to the prairie lands of Alberta.

Mrs. Bjorinson had come with a brave heart, fully determined, no matter what her feelings might be of longing for old and familiar faces and scenes, never to let her family hear one word of discontent.

A tent-house had sheltered them during the spring and summer months. These houses were boards half-way up, with a tent drawn over the top; a board floor to keep them free of dampness; and an outhouse in which to cook. They had been most comfortable while their house was being built and made cozy and warm for the winter. Her husband having a knowledge of masonry had constructed with his own hands a splendid fireplace of stones from near-by. They had been provided with a cow, some chickens and a couple of pigs, for all of which they had plenty of food — prairie grass everywhere.

Coal could be had, some five miles distant, by digging it out of the river bank; while trees of the poplar and small pine made their firewood. Altogether they were well pleased. A quarter of a section of land for themselves, and another set aside for the boy — all for doing the Homestead Duties, or, as familiarly called, "Proving it up."

The days had flown so swiftly that the older Bjorinsons had not given a thought to the eventful day coming nearer with each setting sun, until it was injected into their minds by the sudden question of their boy.

November was already hanging the curtain of night earlier and earlier, until not long after Emil's return from school the sun's last rays could be seen tipping the western highlands.

That evening, as they sat by the dying embers, Mrs. Bjorinson told her husband of Emil's persistent questioning; the night before he had heard the final declarations from the two young members of the household and was amused.

"What are we to do? I would not disappoint the children for the world — and we must think ahead."

"Is there anything we could sell?" asked the father.

"I do not think so; the hens we must not part with; the eggs are so useful for eating."

"No, and we cannot get the money for our grain, it is not yet threshed. Some day we'll have a machine of our own and will not have to wait for one."

"Yes, we surely shall," as she looked wistfully at her husband.

One morning a neighbour brought the mail. A Canadian postmark!

Mrs. Bjorinson.

Dear Friend,

You came to Canada this spring and are one of our New Canadians. We do not want you to be lonely this first Christmas away from your own land.

Our Club has the names of six families in your district who have come to this country recently, and we are sending them something as a welcome to Canada. Please send me the number in your family, boys or girls, and their ages.

Enclosed is an addressed envelope; just put the letter inside, and mail as soon as you can.

Yours very sincerely,

E. L. Kelso,

Sec. C. M. Chapter of the I.O.D.E.

Her heart bounded with joy; now she could tell her son there would be a Jule-Missen, when he came from school. She had scarcely finished answering the note when Emil rushed in, his face beaming with emotion: "Oh! Mother, I came home from school with Nikoli Kronski, and he said there is a Jule-Missen here. He was in Canada last year. He said, they call him Santa Claus here; he's all dressed in red, with a funny cap, and rides right over the tops of the houses, and down the chimney. And, Mother, just think! He said that Santa Claus brought them more than they ever got from Kris Kringle in the land he came from."

"I am so glad you asked your new friend about it, for they had only been here a short time last year, and if he came to them, he will surely come to us this time."

The last day of school had come — two days more, and then Christmas. While the little girl slept, a large parcel arrived and was carefully stowed away out of sight.

Christmas morning dawned fair and bright, but cold. The sun arose over a scene of great beauty, making a million diamonds sparkle on the newly-fallen snow, in the crystalline atmosphere.

Mr. and Mrs. Bjorinson arose early, as was the custom in their native land and though there was no church within reach, they in their own way were keeping the nativity night.

A log fire was burning brightly in the fireplace; in the kitchen the kettle was singing a merry song, as two small figures stole out of the adjoining room. A moment they hesitated, grasped each other round the neck, while from each pair of childish lips came a suppressed, "O-oh!"

Two stockings, full to the top, hung on either side of the fire-place, and below, at a safe distance from the sparks — a hamper. Its contents were marked, "Mr. and Mrs. Bjorinson — A Merry Christmas from the C. M. Chapter of the I.O.D.E. — Calgary."

The December sun had long since gone to rest beyond the horizon, while four happy people sang together their hymn of praise (in their own language) to that heavenly Father for his Christmas blessings.

Two weary children snuggled up to their parents to say good-night, whispering as they did so, "We'll stay now in Canada. Jule-Missen did come; there really is one here, and a better one than we left behind, even if his name is Santa Claus."

.

Emily Spencer Kerby, second row, right, leader of Anti-Knockers Bible Class, 1912. Courtesy of Central United Church, Calgary.

CHAPTER THREE

WOMEN AND THE CHURCH

Between 1914 and 1930, Emily confronted the religious establish-ment. She was a sincere, liberal Christian, who interpreted the teachings of Christ as a source of hope and liberation for women. Never reluctant to meet a challenge head on, she castigated men in her denomination who demonstrated a subtle but destructive and controlling prejudice against women. Using the battle cry of the Christian social activists — "In Christ there is neither Jew nor Greek, bond or free, male or female, all are one" — she claimed equality for women within the Christian community.[1]

Women constituted the majority in the Methodist denomination and were counted on for church support and community work. In spite of this, the male hierarchy continuously barred women from exercising the vote, thus officially limiting female participation in the policy making and direction of the church. In 1914 the campaign to have women admit-ted into full government membership was again defeated. As "A Western Correspondent" Emily responded. She noted that women were useful to the church insofar as they assumed the menial and exhausting tasks del-egated to the "feminine" role. When it came to addressing the issues of social corruption in the world, the men closed the doors and forbade women a voice. Consistently, women were seen as the root of sin and men's sexual transgressions, and they were banned from ordination in most denomi-nations. Emily decried both the subtle and blatant forms of misogyny that were accepted in the church.

---

[1] Paul's letter to the Galatians 3:28. New Testament scripture. There are various interpretations of Paul's teachings on the role of women. The tra-ditional interpretation has been that Paul believed women should keep silent in the assemblies and that men were to be in authority over them. But there is also clear evidence in the New Testament that some women were leaders in the various Christian communities and that Paul recog-nized the significance of their ministry. Indeed, the continuing presence of women as leaders either as nuns, mystics, preachers, or teachers within Christianity is a fact.

"A WEE TINY ROSEBUD"[2]

It was just a little "old fashioned bonnet, with a bit of ribbon on it," and a wee tiny rosebud peeping from under the folds, as though perhaps it was trying to hide among the folds, having a presentiment of the long and lasting trouble it was to cause.

Grandmother was a sweet young girl of the olden school, when women wore their dresses trailing on the ground, after the style of a modern dust mop. True her dress was cut low at the neck, much as in the present day, but as long as her legs were covered, it was all right. We had not progressed far enough to feel that necks were immoral, as we do now; at least by most people.

Women are not bothered, but the modern man seems to be so very sensitive to anything he sees.

I have never been able to understand how any great sculptor could be a man, because statuary is so undressed, he'd have to drape the marble, while he cut and chiseled it — possibly that is why we have so few sculptors today.

But grandmother wore frills and a shawl — the wide-spreading crinoline the faintest showing of her figure.

At night she retired with a big buttermilk plaster on her face, to keep her skin white. Those were the days of sunbonnets and parasols, and the greatest crime a woman could commit was to allow the sun to have a look at her face, not out of consideration for the sun, but her. But we are progressing, nowadays they are so careful on account of the son. Poor son, what a time he has had, ever since in Eden when Adam told Eve to attire herself in a fig-leaf. But there is where she made a mistake. She foolishly did as he suggested, and thus man got the upper hand. And, oh dear! what a time he has had, and still is having to relinquish this age-old grasp, on her dress.

Eve's dress would never do for today. No, never! Her immodest array would be published in every paper in the land. Fig-leaves! Everyone knows how frail they are, they would not stand a whiff of wind until they were gone. But it only goes to prove we always did wear fragile things.

Now, grandmother was all right; so far as her clothes were concerned she conformed to the usual rules of the time — but something else was wrong. A thing she never thought about. She was a bride, and surely brides had some privileges, but alas for grand-

[2] Constance Lynd, "Grandmother's Bonnet," *Calgary Daily Herald,* June 3, 1922, p. 15.

mother! I rather think she was a little proud of her appearance that beautiful spring morning, as she came to the church door to attend the old-time love feast, or quarterly meeting. And who could blame her? This was a ceremony that always bothered me. I did not like it. This was the method of procedure. After the meeting was opened with singing and prayer, a plate was passed round containing small cubes of bread followed by a large mug or bowl of water, out of which all drank in token of our love and fellowship, one with the other.

That fact that many of those who partook had anything but love for each other (especially at election times) did not at all bother me. I was not old enough to fathom such things, but there was something that did trouble me very much. I did not want to drink of out of that mug, after some of the old men, with long moustache and whiskers, had partaken — I did so hate the idea of all the hair around their mouths, often highly coloured with tobacco and chewing tobacco at that, getting into the water. It was wicked, I know, and being a woman, it was decidedly wrong. I early learned, however, that tobacco in any form has never been, or is, an obstacle to "free grace" — or yet to a prospective seat in the upper sanctuary among the saints. It was always a source of contemplation for me that the things men wanted to do were never taboo religiously, but all sorts of restrictions were put upon the female half of creation, and the things she wanted.

Then I learned that men made all the standards of what was right and wrong, and if we failed in the smallest iota, we were doomed. Religion (I do not say Christianity) has always been hard on woman. The men made the standards, and we being "more spiritual" than they, hoped to some time achieve heaven, by their favour, so we fell into line. We believed that God did not think much of women. We were here for one purpose, to make this world nice and homey for the men. I thought that God spoke to them and trusted them, as he never would us. We were a sort of an afterthought. Then, too, the Bible seemed to read that way too, and the preachers were always ringing the changes on the awful peril of "women and wine," so I had a sort of feeling that some day we might be legislated out of existence, like the whiskey, and it behooved us to mind our P's and Q's.

The result was, we became submissively religious, which is always a bad thing. We did the religion, as per pattern, while the men looked on. That is what is the matter with the world today. To use a western expression, the women have "bucked" on doing all the religion. If ever you have seen a western horse buck, you will understand what is the state of our feelings. But that mug! I did not want to drink out of it, so I always hurried and tried to get the front seat, in the hopes that I should drink first out of the one I got, or that passed me. I even hoped that the preacher would forget to take it until after. Usually I was disappointed, for the church has always fostered class distinction. First, the clergy, then the officers, and the privates bringing up the rear.

Women have always (until recently) been privates, with no chance of promotion. They always belonged to the commissariat department. Their duty was to feed the saints, which were always male ones, and good eaters. They might be ever so cranky and crotchety old fellows, that the humble private could not abide, and we often wondered where their sainthood came in. But men said they were saints, and far be it for a member of this department to argue — Saints they must be:

> Theirs not to reason why,
> Theirs not to make reply,
> Theirs but to bake and fry;
> Submissive Commissariat.

It was the quarterly meeting at ten o'clock, in the beautiful month of June. Dressed in all her pretty clothes, she had in those days, grandmother presented herself, together with her newly married husband, at the church door. I fancy I can see her, so sweet and demure, walking along the shady country road to the house of God. The trees were in full bloom, singing their sweet praises to their maker, with the dainty colour of their blossoms, and sweet incense of the perfume of peach tree, apple and hawthorn.

Amidst all this beauty, they reached the door when something happened. No one I feel sure will ever believe what I am going to tell, unless I give my credentials. I am a reliable person. Born in a Methodist parsonage, and raised in the Methodist faith in the time (now happily gone) when each denomination felt that they, and they only, had "the right of way," on the road to the heavenly country. Those were the days when the Presbyterians preached "predestination," the Baptists, "salvation only by the water route," while the Methodists had a wider line "free grace." It sounded wider, but when you got on, you found they were all running on the "narrow gauge." Each was conducting parties to the heavenly country by their own special route. It was always perplexing to me, having a through ticket on the latter road (provided I did not fall off), for the Methodists always made provision for a smash up, or a possible slide down hill.

Had I had the privilege of choosing my own religion, I think I would have chosen the Presbyterian route, as this was provided with safety switches. Once surely on, you were safe from the eternal worry that you were not, or that you might slip off. But in those days you took your religion as you took your parents. You were what you were, just because birth put you there, and to change was as foreign as a summer flower blooming in mid-winder. But what of grandmother's bonnet? Just have patience and I will tell you all about it. It is a real story, and shows how the simple trimming may cause a real catastrophe.

Grandmother was one of the early descendants of the Puritans, who came to this country for "religious liberty," and this they would have at all costs. The first thing they did was to put up restrictions and hedges. They laid great stress on dress, amusements and adorning. So the proper dress for the devout was prescribed. Though they saw the flowers clothed in all their beauty and gorgeousness of colouring, fresh from the hand of God, they failed to read in these the hand marks of a loving Heavenly Father. They saw a chance to "crucify the flesh" by the suppression of colour and brightness of dress. So it was decreed; and the professing Christian of the Methodist order (of the female persuasion) found herself shorn of all the things so dear to her heart. Rules and regulations were laid down, as unalterable as the laws of the Medes and Persians.

Grandmother was a blushing bride in all the glory of her first Sunday at church. It was a great day in which she came under the eyes of the people with whom she was to make her home. This I fancy was the substitute for the society column of the press today.

It was the quarterly love feast, before the communion. This corresponded to the preparation service of the Presbyterian church, which was always held on the Friday before Communion. Being Scotch, it took longer to prepare them — ours soaked in quicker. And grandmother was there in her wedding bonnet. At the door stood a man (there's always a man in such positions); his business was to see that the female members were properly clothed. I never could understand the smallness of the man who could do this, and have so much wrong in his own life, that he somehow seemed to think God took no account of, just kind of winked at because he was a man.

As she was about to enter, the voice of the keeper of the saints' clothing rang out clear and strong, "Mr. Lorry, you may go into

the church, but your wife cannot, she has a flower in her bonnet!"
"If my wife, who is a member of the church, cannot go in because
of a rosebud, then I'll never enter a church as long as I live." Grandfather and his wife went to their home.

Years passed, and to that home there came boys and girls. They
grew up to healthy manhood and womanhood, becoming worthy
citizens of our country. Grandmother, shorn of her rosebud, still
went to church, that she might be an example to her children.
Mothers are so much more careful of this than fathers as a rule. I
wonder why?

It was the days of the circuit rider. The annual conference was
over, and the wheels of revolution had brought to the community
a new preacher. It was the first Sunday morning, and in one of the
old-fashioned pews, as he sat in the pulpit, he saw a young woman
who attracted his attention. Then and there he resolved, "If I can
get her for a wife I will." Of course this was fearfully wicked, or
would have been, had a young woman allowed her thoughts to
stray thus. I tell it — only that you may know you cannot always
be sure of what even a preacher is thinking in the pulpit.

When grandfather heard that his favourite daughter was going to marry a minister (for, of course he got her, for marrying a
minister in those days was equivalent to a passport to heaven hereafter) — when he knew of it, you may imagine his chagrin. Though
grandmother had been gone to the other world for some years, he
was again a young man. He remembered again the old church, his
young bride and the rosebud. To think that his daughter was to be
part of all this. Yes, he had made a vow, and he would keep it. He
would not consent to the marriage taking place in his house, and
all on account of a rosebud. Had grandfather been a professing
member of the church such obstinacy then would have been considered "great religious strength," but not being so, it was labeled
just common "cussedness." I do not know whether I should tell
you or not, but in the years that followed he was a cripple. I can
fancy I hear some of the sanctimonious ones say, "God's judgment
on him." By no means. Only ordinary carelessness of an old man
on the ice — personally I have found ice is just as slippery whether
it is saint or sinner on it.

In the declining years of life, this son and daughter were his
greatest comfort and joy, then when at last the spirit had taken its
everlasting flight, it was June again. In his folded hands was a
rosebud. It had kept him out of the church militant, but — did it
keep him out of the church triumphant?

"PLEASE SOMEONE ... EXPLAIN 'FEMININITY' "[3]

And so again we are turned down by our brothers, the professed followers of the Christ, in whose kingdom there is neither "male nor female, bond nor free." These men have a long way to go yet, to get the meaning of the "kingdom of God." In spite of this declaration, they persist in recognizing male and female, and in being responsible for much of the bondage of women today. If these men (no doubt very wise) would read the signs of the times they would seize the moment to show their progressiveness, and in years to come it might be said of them "they were men of vision." Instead, future generations, reading the minutes of the General Conference of 1914, will laugh over their old fogyism, and their denseness. How afraid these dear brethren are of us "losing our femininity." Never mind, when we lose it, some of the men we know can supply the demand. What do these men mean [by] "femininity"? Just this: to act as they think we should act — do the things they say — to be interested only in what they prescribe.

In fact, man has set our limits, and when we step beyond, we lose our "femininity." In other words, we educated women translate the dear sweet word "femininity" to mean "fool." We have been living in a world where as women we have been fools, but now, having attained the age of sight, we can no longer be soothed to sleep by the gush and slush about "our influence." Our influence has been great, and is greater today than ever, but we are waking up to find that with it all, the liquor traffic and the white slave traffic, are still with us. "Influence" has not succeeded in doing away with them. These things are run by men for men and women pay the price.

The men in our city are not quaking for our femininity. We have the franchise. If we pay rent or own property — even if we get married, we are not supposed to have lost our brains, though I must confess when I see the kind of men some women marry, I am not surprised that they lose their vote, and Toronto recognizes this evidently, in manipulating the franchise for women as she has in the past. [4]

But having been a church worker for years, I am at a loss to know what the dear brethren mean by "losing our femininity." No

---

[3] PAA, 75.387 (UCCA-AC), Box 181, Item 6029, A Western Correspondent, "The Women and Our Church Courts," clipping, publication unknown, 1914.

[4] At that time women in Toronto did not have the municipal vote as did their sisters in Calgary.

65

men, even the pastors, ever feared we women would "lose our femininity" when tea-meeting time came round, and we hugged and tugged at heavy tables, and got them in place, and lifted the heavy boilers of coffee and potatoes, etc., etc. No layman, or pastor stood round and declared their fears of us losing our femininity. And yet, I must confess, many a day, after the strain and stress of such work, I've felt I've lost everything, soul in the bargain, trying to keep my temper sweet in the midst of such surroundings. But then a soul is a small thing compared to "femininity." Will the dear brother who made this remark please explain what "femininity" is. Really, I am so ignorant I want light. Personally I would like to see what the church would do, if the women of Canada withdrew their support and help for just one month. I have found the lifting tea-meetings tables, etc., etc., far more of a stress on my physical, mental and moral makeup than having a ride in a motor car, with five or six other ladies, to the polling booth, and dropping my ballot in the box — then a drive home again, and the men most gracious to us, because we have the power of the ballot. Wake up men of the Methodist Church, or we may play you a trick that will be worth two of yours.

Please, someone, preferably the "dear brother," explain "femininity."

"GOOD, JOLLY BROTHERS" VERSUS SUFFRAGE[5]

To the Editor of the *Christian Guardian*:

Dear Sir: In your issue of March 17th, I noticed an editorial [that] read: "It is practically certain that there will be no immediate extension of the municipal franchise to married women in the Province of Ontario, but the debate on the question is interesting enough." The editor states the "proposition is so eminently reasonable, and so mildly progressive" — quite ladylike, you know — "that it is a marvel the government should hesitate in this matter." Then the editor tells us that about the "only argument against it was that it was a step in the direction of woman suffrage," and that the "organized liquor traffic, with its great wealth and voting strength, is the chief argument against woman suffrage" in Ontario today. But, Mr. Editor, you forget that the organized Methodist Church with its great wealth and wisdom and its peculiar political methods, last autumn was as equally opposed to granting

[5] Constance Lynd, "No Votes for Married Women," *Christian Guardian*, April 14, 1915, p. 27.

woman any position of advancement — viz., equality with her brother — in the church courts. And when this "interesting debate" in the Ontario Legislature took place, and at which no doubt many of the same good brethren were present, one of the chief arguments used was the fact that the legislative assembly of the great Methodist Church considered its women *non compos mentis* [not of sound mind]. So I don't think the Church need put it over on the liquor traffic; they are simply hand in hand — good, jolly brothers, you know. "A common cause makes brothers of us all."

"PAUL WAS A VICTIM OF CUSTOM"[6]

Today, the ever present question is being asked, "What is the matter with the Church?" The answer is not far to seek. The Church has always been governed by precedent. There is no harder link to break than this old link when once forged.

The women in the Anglican Church (this time) are asking for greater privilege in church services, and one of the more progressive of the dignitaries argues, "if it is only custom that is hindering, then custom *must be broken*."

Strange, isn't it, how men swear by Paul and forget all about what Christ said? Paul was a victim of custom. He had never been used to see[ing] women at church, save with a mantle or shawl over their heads. It was the proper thing in those days, as in many eastern countries today. Then why don't the ministers, to be perfectly Pauline, insist on the shawls over our heads today?

"Drink no longer water," says Paul, "but use a little wine for thy stomach's sake, and thine other infirmities." Yet the church preaches prohibition.

"Suffer not the women to teach." How does the church reconcile this flagrant breach of Paul's command, in view of the day and Sunday Schools which would be closed were the women to leave them?

And yet I believe in the Church. But if the woman or the autocrats must go, let it be the autocrats.

If democracy means anything, it means all, and not even the church can hold an autocratic attitude and belong to the great democracy.

"Let the women keep silence in the church, for it is not permitted unto them to speak." He does not say God said so — just Jewish custom.

---

[6] Constance Lynd, "Paul, The Preachers and The Women," *Woman's Century*, April, 1920, p. 32.

Then again —"If a woman would learn anything let her ask her husband." But what of the women who have none? Also what of those who know more than their husbands?

Women kept silence so long that men let the world get rife with liquor, prostitution and specific disease. Women wondered what was wrong; then they suddenly stopped asking men for knowledge and got to work in school and university and hospital.

"The head of the man is Christ." True. That's inspired. Man here means the race both male and female. But Paul also says, "the head of *every woman* is the man," and that sentence has rung down the ages and stultified womanhood and kept her back for centuries.

"A woman must not have authority over a man." Yet we find women today directing men. If she knows a job better, why not? And Queen Victoria was a woman.

"God created man (the race) in his own image . . . male and female created he them, and said . . . replenish the earth and subdue it." This was spoken to the two. Yet in spite of all these utterances, Paul himself has said, "In Christ there is neither male nor female, but all are one."

O men of the church of all denominations! Listen! Forget the old Jewish ideas about women, as you forget about the wine and the shawls and the women's teaching. Be big enough to get the larger viewpoint.

"In Christ there is neither male nor female, but all are one."

"I BELIEVE"[7]

We cannot solve 20th century problems with a 16th century creed; cannot face modern issues with doctrines of the Middle Ages. These people wrote the Creed for their times. It is our duty to carve our own Creed out of the living, vital issues of the day in which we live.

1. I believe in <u>Home</u> as the foundation of the Kingdom of God.
Child learns love of God in Mother's love.
Every mother is a possible Mary.
Every father a possible Joseph.
Every babe a possible Messiah.

2. I believe in my <u>Community</u> — in playgrounds that will build health in blood of child; in schools, public libraries, that will answer

---

[7] PAA, 75.387 (UCCA-AC), Box 181, Item 6027, Emily Spencer Kerby, "My Creed," n.d.

youth's quest for Truth; in social centres, Y.M.s and Y.W.s to give moral direction to life; in the Christian Church, that gives organized and institutional expression to the Christ spirit. I believe that Beauty and Health can be built into a city's life: slums into beautiful homes, swamps into gardens and parks, filthy rivers into clear streams, dark alleys into well lighted boulevards.

3. I believe in the onward march of <u>Industry</u> and <u>Commerce</u>. I believe wealth was meant for public service; that Labour and Capital must be interpreted in terms of common good. If Labour and Capital will approach each other in Christian spirit, it will mean the triumph of Justice and Brotherhood.

4. I believe in our age of <u>Scientific Discoveries and Inventions,</u> and when we learn to combine these with Christ's spirit of good will, the Kingdom of God will come with POWER.

5. I believe in all men is [the] instinct of <u>Brotherhood</u>; that at the heart of the Universe there is a great Love, that is international and super-racial; a love that is destined to "beat swords into plowshares and spears into pruning hooks."

I believe that war is a curse — robs mothers of their sons, sends the most vigorous to an early grave, retards industrial progress, destroys the world's finest works of art, brutalizes men, and is followed by disease, famine, plague and death, and that it will eventually be defeated by the Spirit of Christ. I believe there is a <u>Spirit</u> at work in the world, a spirit of universal sympathy, universal justice, universal brotherhood, that will eventually bring international peace in every corner of the globe, and all men are called to unite with the living God, who is working for the triumph of righteousness and peace.

6. I believe in <u>Christ</u>; in the winsomeness of his character; in the beauty of his moral teaching; in the loyalty of his cause; in his triumphant faith; in his willingness to lay down his life for the redemption of the people. I believe the God who moved in the background of his life will work through you and me.

7. I believe in the <u>Immortality of the Soul</u>. I believe that a man may build himself into the Kingdom of God in this world; that he may become strong in his inner life with a vigorous spiritual faith; that:

no nail in his hand.
no bullet through his heart,
no spear in his side,
no germ of disease,
can destroy his unconquerable Soul.

8. I believe that God is the indwelling, fatherly presence, "who is nearer to us than breathing, closer than hands or feet"; that heaven begins in this world. I believe in the teeming life of spring time, colours of autumn, unfolding flowers, singing birds, in the cry of the dumb brute, in the majesty of the spreading tree, the laughter of children, in the prayers of a mother, in youth's quest for truth and life, in the struggle of men for justice and brotherhood, in the daily call of duty, in the inner light of truth and the whisper of the still, small voice — in all, God is mysteriously present, and eager to inspire men today, as ever before.

"YE GODS! DO I WAKE OR AM I DREAMING?"[8]

To the Editor of the *New Outlook*:

Dear Sir, lest women in general who read the above mentioned article in the last issue of the *Chatelaine* should be misled by it, may I be allowed to challenge some of the unfounded statements for the sake of the women of Canada.[9] It is due them.

What womanhood is asking is not some corner in the sanctuary where she may "appropriately render service," but *freedom* to work where she deems best. It is not an entirely new thing; there are a number of ordained women ministers on this mundane sphere.

Why should there be such dire calamity follow the granting of justice she asks? "A capable, godly, well-trained woman, meeting all the requirements laid down for a man minister for ordination" — and here's the rub — she isn't a male.

Why should her ability to teach "doctrine" be questioned? A man-made thing after all; and rather out of fashion in this twentieth

---

[8] Constance Lynd, "Women and the Ministry: Constance Lynd Replies to Dr. Ernest Thomas," letter to the Editor, *New Outlook*, November 7, 1928, pp. 18, 20.
[9] Ernest Thomas, "Women in the Pulpit and in the Innermost Sanctum," *Chatelaine*, October, 1928, pp. 6-7 and 52. Thomas was a prominent United Church Minister who opposed the full ordination of women because of their sexual allurement and how males in congregations would react to an attractive female preacher.

century; it has gone the way of the tallow candle, the idea of a flat earth, as well as the fable that man (the male) was "lord of creation."

If, as the writer says, "There was in considering the ordination of women a great lack of high and serious discussion" — there has not been any lack on woman's part of high thinking. It is simply a masculine prejudice, which will and must go, ere woman achieves the place God gave her in the dawn of creation: "male and female created He them, and said unto them, 'have dominion over the earth and subdue it,'" — and further attested by the Christ: "there is neither male nor female."

"Influence" is not what women are seeking; they have been lulled into sleep by the platitudes surrounding that word for centuries. It is not "influence," but justice; not power but freedom of choice. As long as women do not have this, they are slaves — and the worst of slavery is that "it breeds the soul of a slave."

Once our high schools were closed to women — the universities, the professions, men fought against the release of these things for women, but it came. They said, "No one will ever employ a woman doctor or a woman lawyer," but they do.

Women are laughing in derision at the statement, "That within the Roman Communion ... feminism has found its earliest and fullest development." Feminism is not what we are seeking, only fair play. Nor are Protestant women yet willing to abide by the "timely reminder" of the papal utterance that "feminism" (how we hate that word) — "feminism" does not depend on this project. It is not "feminism" or any other ism we are seeking, but liberty.

Such blindness! — to offer "the extending of influence" in the Church courts in lieu of ordination. Mark you! it is still that sweetest of words, "Influence." It is the old story. "I asked for bread, and you gave me a stone." But it will come, *the ordination*, when the real light of Christ's love breaks in on the Church.

Then Dr. Thomas says: "The enfranchisement of women did not cause any spectacular change in affairs." Why should it? Did it when men achieved the universal manhood franchise? — for even they did not always have it; though they would have us believe that even in the Garden of Eden, Adam was the only person at the ballot box. How tame! We would like to remind the writer that the great things, the big things of life, the things which make history, move quietly: "God was not in the wind, the storm or the thunder, but in the still small voice."

71

Woman has always had "creative power" — they are the race; it is through them the race flows; what enfranchisement did for her, was what it did for man, when he achieved it by bitter fight. It gave her the sense of dignity and equality.

Had the writer of said article lived in the West in earlier times he would never have made such a statement as "that the advent of women in the electorate had made no marked political change." No; but they made changes and *marked* changes. Here women and girlhood had no legal protection, for property, for the husband leaving every mite of his property away from his wife and children.[10] The heart of women ached for their sisters, less fortunate, as they tried by that blessed word "influence" to secure changes to the laws. The powers-that-be listened to them mayhap politely, and showed them out, with perhaps the consoling words: "We'll take this into consideration." Any man or woman in this day knows what that means. It is never heard from.

What a change when womanhood had achieved the right to go before Governments with her wishes, and say: "We want this law passed." See the result, and then say that the "enfranchisement of women made no marked change, or more correctly, made no marked change in the *political situation*. We asked [for] the vote, not for *politics*, — but for humanitarian reasons.

To woman's credit in the West-land we have as follows: 1. Mother's Pensions; 2. Woman's Home Protection Act; 3. The Devolution of Estates Act; 4. Age of consent raised to eighteen; 5. Marriage licenses sold in the Courthouse; 6. Women's courts for women; 7. The right of custody of a woman's own child; 8. Marriage age raised to sixteen.

To the shame of man, it has been as low in places as twelve — and we Christians talk of the horrors of India — stop! — think! Prior to this, the woman who had gone through the pangs of childbirth that a child might live had no legal claim to her own child. Will any one agree with Dr. Thomas that women have made no "marked change"? Sheer ignorance.

We wanted power and equality, and got it. Some four years ago we went to the Federal House. We had the right, we were voters. The request was backed by 400,000 women of Canada. To

---

[10] Until the passage of the Dower Act in 1917, wives and/or daughters in Alberta were not guaranteed property rights even though they would have, in most rural areas, worked alongside the man whose name was on the land title, to establish the farm, ranch or business.

the credit of the House at that time they passed all. The Senate blocked them all. In the first case we had power; in the second we had "influence" only. The Senate cared nothing for our request; they are not voted into office, but appointed for life.

It is an insult to the women of Canada to state: "There were priestesses in the pagan religions, and we must hesitate before giving under the Christian religion such a place to women." We can say Amen to that. Does the writer think the educated women of this day do *not know exactly what* these women priestesses were? No Protestant Church has ever had a woman to confess to. The "psychological facts" as spoken of are mere ghosts, and phantoms of the mind.[11]

Here's a hard one! I quote, "Prejudices are labor-saving aids to practical living." Grant it; then it is a wonder that men, with all their devotion to custom, tradition, doctrine, and prejudice have ever survived the inventions of the age.

We seem to see them still trudging behind the ancient plough; eschewing the reaper, or combine — hauling water with a windlass, scorning the motor car, and reading their Bibles by the guttering light of a tallow candle. Their *devotion* at this time to tradition would be *startling*, were it not so supremely funny.

Then, the "power of an attractive woman preacher, with all her *subtle sex appeal*" and from the Church! Ye gods! Do I wake or am I dreaming? Is this the sixteenth century, or the year of our Lord 1928?

"The masked symptoms" — we leave to those who understand — we do not.

When women speak of handsome men they say: "a fine personality, attractive appearance in the pulpit," all assets for a man; but in a woman! — a danger to the common masculine good.

Dr. Thomas gives rebirth to an ancient idea that a beautiful woman "was and is always a temptress." We rather prided ourselves it was dead, decently buried and turned to dust; witness its resurrection!

Lastly, as the preachers say, "The supreme corporate act of the Church in the Holy Communion *has been* always restricted to men." Has been is never a *reason* for anything; lots of has beens of the past have become *are* today.

---

[11] Thomas refers to the "psychological fact" that women as leaders within the church do not have the same authority as males to forgive sins. He claimed that most women would shrink from the idea of confessing to a female priest.

"The presence of a few women in the ranks of the ministry will have slight effect." We agree with him that "the remark is irrelevant," — adding also *trite*. It is not the effect on the ministry we are concerned about, it is the effect on women, and on the outposts of civilization; the fifty-two vacant spots where there are no services; this and not the ministry is at stake, but the far flung hamlets of our Canada.

"WOMEN — THE VERY BEST OF CHURCH WORKERS"[12]

I cannot say with the Psalmist: "Now I am old, yet have I not seen the righteous forsaken, nor his seed begging bread."

Women are the seed of the righteous, equally with men. They have been begging years and years for the bread of equality and the freedom of life, or if you like, self-determination.

A Great One said, "There is neither male nor female." Twenty centuries have almost passed since these words were spoken, yet today we find discrimination against women — the very best of church workers.

Why in the discussion of the place of women in the church should sex enter at all? If she is fit to give birth to men, to care for them, train them — and to preach — is she not deemed fit to administer the sacrament or marry? If we are morally unfit to administer — then we are not fit to take.

Every church has had its misfits; in the ministry there is no "corner" on such in any denomination; and we women have taken the sacrament from these unknowingly at times.

In some of our provinces the man who sells the licenses has the right to marry all who come to him and there is no question ever asked regarding it as to fitness or the propriety of the matter.

Only three places are closed to woman now. She may enter every profession equally with her brother man — save the *Senate*, the *Ministry* and the *beer parlors*. This should surely give the great United Church food for thought.

We are glad to see that one man at least has seen the light in the person of Rev. Samuel Rose, D.D.[13] In the last issue of the *New*

---

[12] PAA, 75.387 (UCC-AC), Box 181, Item 6028. Constance Lynd, "Tired of Being a Woman," clipping, publication unknown, December 29, 1928.

[13] The Rev. Dr. Rose was a United Church minister, and the *New Outlook* was the United Church magazine. There had been a series of articles written by ministers on the issue of female ordination.

Outlook he says — "I would as cheerfully accept the cup from the hands of a godly woman as an Archbishop."

The Church today should take thought and see whither tending.

The Church today is not dealing with the woman of ten centuries ago, but with the modern twentieth-century woman — an educated, reading, thinking woman, and a "not-afraid-to-express-her opinion woman" of the year 1928.

"WIMMIN AND WINE"[14]

It is the phrase that has rung down the ages.

Diaphonus' oratory flings into our faces the warning against "wine and wimmin."

Women wince under it, yet few of them ever take the trouble to think of the real basic cause for the use of it.

Adam was supposed to have fallen through "wimmin," but from personal observation of Adam's sons, I am inclined to think the writer of the story fabricated.

Anyway that started the whole rumpus. It's easy to start a thing but mighty hard to stop it.

Next thing we hear is Noah drunk in his tent, and a complication with "wimmin." That finished the job, and from that time on speakers and writers even today rail against "wine and wimmin" as the first cause of man's undoing, little realizing they are putting the outward manifestation for the inside of the man.

The real cause lies within.

Later we get the Jewish law, as written by Moses, where one, reading carelessly and without thought, would imagine women were something to be shunned, because of the frequent reoccurrence of the word "unclean."

Such was not the case. These were the great God-given health laws, for the protection of womanhood, in an age that had no knowledge of the human body. This idea was projected into much of the more modern religions, [and has] given woman the name of a "temptress."

In the story of the "White Cowl" we have the theme of a young priest imbued with this idea. He meets for the first time a young woman, and holds conversation with her.

A storm breaks over the country, and he and she are forced into a little schoolhouse for protection. He is surprised to find her

---

[14] Constance Lynd, "Wimmin and Wine," *Woman's Century*, November, 1920, p. 5.

so interesting and well educated and refined. There, while the elements raged (as he thought) in denunciation of his pleasure in conversing with her, he finds the truth for himself that she is sweet and pure as the driven snow — savors nothing of a "temptress," but is such as the gods favor — an "angel in disguise."

Next we find David committing murder to get another man's wife for himself. Note, she was innocent of it all. Then follows his son, Solomon, with his seven hundred wives and three hundred concubines whom we are told "he loved," and that they turned him away from God to idols. Honestly, what man with seven hundred wives could have any time for God. He was away from God before he ever got the seven hundred, but — blame the "wimmin."

What was at the bottom of all this? Adam said, "The woman tempted me, and I did eat," and we believed it. But I notice he got a good steady job to keep him out of mischief.

We have no proof that Solomon's wives tempted him, but it does say, Solomon loved many strange "wimmin." And he's not the last man has done the same, though I'm not sure about the "love." There was something wrong with Noah when he took the wine and got drunk. There was something wrong with David and Solomon (inside), and with every other man who says the "wimmin" tempt me.

One day a man came into the Manse where I was visiting. He was deeply concerned because he had come across some peculiar sect, professing greater holiness than the rest of us poor mortals who had told him he could not be "holy and wear a pair of tan boots" he had purchased. "It was worldly," they were fashionable then.

The pastor told him he need not trouble him[self]; if that was all that kept him from holiness he thought he was pretty safe. Then he told the minister confidentially that the boots did not trouble him, he'd give them up easily — but that his upsetting sin was "wimmin," and he was a man of sixty.

To all such let me advise to read, "What a Man of Forty-five Ought to Know." He was ready and willing to part with the shoes, but the "wimmin!"

So on down the ages we come, and Timothy is warned by his mother against "wimmin and wine" — and we've been getting it ever since, "wimmin and wine," "wimmin and wine," until we're sick of the way men whine about the "wimmin and wine."

Once we as women were classed with Indians, infants and idiots. We've outgrown that. Will the time ever come when educated men will cease calling us a sin and classing us with wine? There are bad women just as there are bad men — but I doubt if [woman] first took the initiative. But when once she has fallen — she sinks low and lower — there is so little comeback for her, while he goes free.

May the day soon come when we'll hear no more of "wimmin and wine" because the wine will be banished from our midst, and "wimmin" we can't banish, but we hope for a day when the men will realize the trouble is in themselves.

The flesh is triumphing over the soul. What would men think if we women were constantly harping on this to their girls — in every public gathering, where social welfare was discussed — Keep away from "wine and men" — "wine and men"? Mind, I am not saying it would be a bad thing to do. I can see there are some who perhaps need the warning to leave the wine alone, if they are to protect themselves against the latter. But to be everlastingly classed with wine — Ah! "that's the rub."

It's no wonder we find young boys despising womanhood — belittling their sisters, and even speaking disparagingly of [their] own mother[s]. Why not? "Wimmin and wine" accounts for it. Men know perfectly well that the law of God is written in their own hearts and bodies.

Let our speakers no longer hold us up to our sons and coming generations as a sin. Let them preach righteousness, purity, as the foundation of manhood.

God knows we're sinned against enough and preyed upon. Don't brand us with "wine." Take these two sentences:

"Look not upon the wine when it is red," etc.

"Whoso looketh upon a woman," etc.

Read these two passages from the Book of books, and see whether it is the "wine and wimmin" who are at fault — or — is it the looking.

Alberta women at the Legislature in Edmonton during passage of the Equal Suffrage Bill, 1916. Emily is possibly in the upper right corner with the massive hat. GAA, NC 6 1002-1.

CHAPTER FOUR

PERSPECTIVES

Emily reflected the views of many middle-class women of the time, and each view was rooted in the values of the society and community that she understood. She spoke of double standards in law, the devastation of venereal disease, the need for birth control and eugenics, and for women's financial and intellectual freedom. She even favoured the liberating changes in women's clothing of the 1920s, although she also emphasized the primary importance and dignity of the mother.

Careers of all kinds were important to her, and she believed that each woman should feel a sense of worth through her life's work. Marriage itself was a career to be entered into more seriously than society had traditionally stressed.

She feared the massive immigration of foreigners whose large families threatened the status quo. Like many others in her society, she accepted the eugenics argument that advocated sterilization of the mentally unfit as a necessary form of population control among those deemed defective.

"THE PASSING OF THE SERVANT IN THE HOME"[1]

There is, perhaps, no greater evidence of the advancement of woman than the fact she has, at last, taken hold of that old and much discussed problem of the "domestic helper."

It has long been used as an argument of derision against the advancement of women in general that she had never yet settled the "servant" question, or learned how to treat those in subordinate positions in life. All honour is due the baby province of our Dominion that she is the first to take hold of this really difficult problem, and has undertaken to deal with it, perhaps feebly for the present and gropingly, but later on, as the work develops and grows, and our vision widens, we shall be able to step out on the solid ground

---

[1] Constance Lynd, "The Passing of the Servant in the Home," *Woman's Century*, Special Number - September, 1918, p. 37.

of experience and place the helpers in our homes where they ought to be. It is not an easy task, nor one that will be easily adjusted, but it is one that is well worth the trying, for the sake of what it will mean to the future both of womanhood and childhood. That the new movement was coming was clear from the observations of the developments in other lines of life, and the evident dissatisfaction among the workers themselves as well as the employers. When these two streams conflict, then look out for trouble or change.

Once the nursing of our sick was confined entirely to the family and friends of the ailing one, except in cases of confinement, when some elderly woman "with experience," did duty, often in exceedingly primitive fashion, when viewed in the light of present day knowledge. The lady in question was not a particularly respected member of society where she lived. In the sixties and seventies of the past century, she was a prolific pedlar of all the neighbourhood gossip. One in particular whom we have in mind, and the only one in a town of some three thousand of a population, we can see yet — black woollen skirt, paisley shawl, and an old time poke-bonnet which covered a head, the like of which could not be found for harbouring, incubating, enlarging and embellishing everything she saw or heard in the various homes in which she served. She was the wholesale and retail news dealer of the community — in fact, she was the daily press, the weekly, and the monthly magazine combined.

Then came a period of training and educating our girls in the hospitals for private work in the homes. Oh, what a commotion was raised because the nurse would not cook and sweep, wash and iron, etc., etc., as her predecessor had done! But people soon found that there was so much woven into her work that was unknown to her forerunner, and it was so different from anything ever seen before, that she was soon accorded a place in society, the place she had made for herself.

What shall we say of the servant! Unfortunately, the word applied to the class who help in our homes has done untold harm; we have applied it to one class of workers when we should have applied it to all.

The merchant is the servant of his customers, the doctor is the servant of his patients, the teacher is the servant of his pupils, the lawyer is the servant of his clients, the clergyman is the servant of his congregation, and so on, through the whole of life. We are indissolubly bound together, as servant and served, in a chain that no one can break no matter how he may try. It matters not what our bank account may be; while money may give us luxury and position to a certain extent, yet, "the mind is the measure of the man," and in any true democracy there must be a levelling up of life on the one true and only basis — that of character and efficiency.

The application of the name "servant" to one class and only one has been responsible for the formation of a caste, as rigid as any caste of India. If a young woman of good abilities succeeds through marriage or effort, in passing from this class to another, however often you will hear the disdainful remark, "Well, she was only a servant before."

The word "servant" still has the onus of bye-gone days, not just being lifted to the place Christ gave it when He said, "If any one would be great among you, let him be your servant."

The war is bringing a reform in this particular (along with many other reforms), perhaps a decade earlier than it would have done.

What has led to it? The utter disruption of European society. From the old families of England, whose servants were born, reared, served and died on the estates, and for whom there was not such a thought as progress or change, many a retainer has gone to the front and into the trenches, where he has fought for freedom alongside his master, and in so doing has realized mayhap for the first time, that he too was a man, with all the desires for freedom of those in other stations of life.

Never again can the old order prevail, and we must set ourselves to working out new plans and schemes for the new age on which we are entering. The "servant" must go, but in her place will come the "trained worker" able and competent, educated and refined, the equal of any and the inferior of none.

The "Housekeepers' Association" of Calgary is the first movement in this direction.[2] It is a long way from the quill pen to the

[2] The Housekeepers' Association in Calgary was formed by women who worked as domestics. The purpose of this Association was to establish domestic work as a profession, to stop exploitation of female workers, and to gain recognition, respect and protection for its members. Women who were "domestic workers" were to have set work hours, wear uniforms, undergo certified training, and live away from their employer. In Calgary these ideals were generally supported by middle-class women as the city continually experienced a shortage of domestic workers. Immigrant single women who had arrived in Canada as domestics were usually offered work as soon as they landed at the Port of Montreal, en route to the West. In Calgary, the Housekeepers' Association attempted to entice these women to Alberta.

typewriter, from the stagecoach to the aeroplane. Still, the type-writer and the aeroplane came; and though this organization may not reach its definite goal today, yet it is blazing the pathway for the women who shall follow.

The "Housekeepers' Association" is a group of workers who have banded themselves together to elevate their work and themselves — in other words, they are seeking freedom. They meet weekly at the Young Women's Christian Association for study, for Red Cross work, and for an insight into literature. Once a month they meet for business. Here they are learning to think and act for themselves, gaining a confidence and self-reliance they have never known before. Their course of study is to extend over two years, when, after passing examinations, they will receive a diploma as a guarantee of their efficiency.

As women employers of help in our homes we have never demanded a definite standard of work. "Strong and willing to work" has been too often sufficient ground for engaging a girl. Then, with infinite patience (more often without it), we have set ourselves to the laborious task of teaching her. After a girl has passed through several homes, with various methods of work, she had as many ways of doing things as a centipede has legs. No man would engage an office help in this way. He demands knowledge and capability. Watch a busy man engaging a stenographer. He tests her the first few days, and if she is not competent he tells her to go — and rightly. Such a thing as teaching her never occurs to him. But why this difference? Because women have never as a whole demanded efficiency, and there has never, until now, been put in their hands the means for securing it.

There is no doubt we women have been to blame for the conditions. We have been too lax in our requirements, and often too small and mean in our dealings with girls. True, there are many miserably poor servants, but we have ourselves to blame to a very great extent.

The teaching of Household Science in our schools, right up to our universities, the making of it as decent a subject of study as German, French, Latin or mathematics, in fact, the counting it as a science, has of itself lifted the work and the worker to another sphere. The servant of today is keen enough to know this, and is preparing for what she sees coming. Girls are graduating from our high schools and from our universities with as perfect a knowledge of this science as of any other. What is going to happen? In the future, a girl will step out of these institutions of learning, and she will often be the superior of her mistress, in her knowledge of both practical and theoretical sides of her work. The girl will be free to choose her vocation in life, and it will be as respectable to work in a home as in a store or office.

The home worker of the future will not live in the home of her employer; she will live in her own home, or in a community house, as does the clerk, the dressmaker, the stenographer, or the teacher. She will do her day's work and return at night, as other employees do, when her time will be her own absolutely.

"With such a programme for our help, how are we ever to get out [for] an evening, for parties, theatres, or amusement?" I hear the frightened housewife ask. Why, you'll simply hire someone, and pay her for her time as in any other walk of life. The old-time servant is going and will go, in the natural order of events, but something better will come to the mothers in the home who must have help, and who today find competent help so difficult to get. The day is not far distant when we shall look back and laugh over the struggles of the past and rejoice in the new order of things. For we must always remember that life is progressive. Stagnation means death. Life is ever better further on. If not, then all efforts would be futile.

"PLAGUE SPOT ON THE RACE"[3]

Woman is the guardian of the race, and for the sake of the race, she must seek the highest good for the child. No woman is doing this as long as she permits even one child to be ill-born if she can prevent it.

"Behold I have set thee as a watchman upon the walls of Zion" used to be thought to mean the preachers, but it also means every woman who sees a little child afflicted — lame — blind — epileptic — deformed — to ask why? And if she will not, or does not, get a true answer, in the last great day she shall hear, "Depart from Me, for I was lame, blind, epileptic, and ye did not help me."

There is no subject of which women in general are so ignorant, and none of which they care to know so little (because they deem it "not nice to discuss such things," yet there is none which more vitally affects woman, her home, and her children, than this very thing.

Venereal disease is something many of our women cannot get away from, no matter how much they may endeavour to escape,

---

[3] Constance Lynd, "The Social Evil," *Woman's Century*, August, 1919, p.16.

and no disease is working greater havoc amongst women than this disease. When will women learn that the normal processes of life are perfectly healthy, but prostitute these and nature — that inexorable judge — makes us pay the penalty.

Women in the past were stupidly content with their position in the world as being "cared for and protected by men," till one day a woman found out she was neither the one nor the other.

There has been some reason for our ignorance in the past, and for this we are excused, but now that some of our nurses and doctors are combining to educate us, the woman who deliberately turns away from knowledge so vital to the race is not worthy of the name of woman. Is it not better to know the causes which have been at work to bring into your home the blind child — that no more may come? Is it not better to know why your child died in infancy of a disease you could not understand and which the doctor called by a long sounding name, and your next, and your next went the same way? Is it right that women should go through the agonies of childbirth to bring forth a being doomed from its first day to early death or a life of misery?

I hear some women say, "My children are all right — why should I care, it is not my concern." It is. Can you not realize that your girl, of whom you are so proud, may marry someone afflicted with this dread disease? Your stalwart son, [of] whom you have boasted, may marry a girl similarly afflicted — then what? You'll never know what. So we cannot put it all down to the husbands. The average doctor won't tell you, and certainly the nurse won't. When doctors tell us that ninety percent of all abdominal operations on women are caused from venereal disease — usually produced from a husband so afflicted, is it not time that, for the sake of womanhood, we should know, and know, act?

I said — knowledge is power — doctors won't tell, not the average ones; they are more concerned as to their professional etiquette than the welfare of the child, but there are an ever increasing number of physicians who are breaking through their crust of medical etiquette and are telling.

We've grown tired of men thinking they can "sow their wild oats" and reap a harvest of pure wheat. What they sow they reap, and if only they alone reaped it would not be so bad, but our girls are sharing the reaping, and generations yet unborn will reap to their sorrow.

We, as women, must become conversant with all the forms of this disease. We must destroy it root and branch. Women must learn that it is just as possible for a man to live a virtuous life as a woman. The seventh commandment was not given to women, but to the whole race of humanity. The idea that man must prostitute the functions of life is an ancient and worn out fable, which no reputable physician today believes, and when our laws make adultery a crime, sure to be punished, without any ifs and buts, men will set themselves to work changing their viewpoint, and learn self-control, as women have learned it. For a woman to be impure was and is a disgrace — for a man to be impure is thought by many (both men and women) to be a virtue.

But the day is not far distant when women all over our dominion will vote and, with the help of good men, will relegate this awful scourge from our midst. We register and isolate scarlet fever, smallpox, diphtheria, measles and mumps, and let the most loathsome and dangerous one walk on our streets.

Women won't face a problem that is not a popular one with the rank and file of men, because womanhood considers itself too nice to talk of such things. True, womanhood is motherly and must and will face every problem for the sake of the child, and be it woman or be it man, the offender must be "brought to book" and a single standard of morality — which the "Woman's Century" has always stood for — must become an understood thing in the community.

There is a strong feeling abroad that "the woman" is to blame; there is a strong feeling growing that "the men" are to blame. Neither are wholly right, neither are wholly wrong — the problem before us is this — are we going to allow a plague spot to ruin the race? Will clean, healthy, splendid physiques amongst our boys and girls become obsolete? — some historical tale told of beautiful men and women who lived some long time ago — but can be seen now-a-days so rarely. Are we coming to this? Has it arrived? Surely not — we will redeem the nation — we will face the problem — we will teach our people that God made them to be temples, with the "beauty of holiness" (and therefore wholeness) shining through their bodies, and all thoughts connected with parenthood as the holy of holies.

"WOMEN'S INDEPENDENCE FOR THE SAKE OF THE RACE"[4]

There is no more pathetic page of history than that which relates the struggle of woman toward industrial life.

The building up of woman's position in the world has been made an almost hopeless failure in the past, because of wrong foundations.

Though woman was the first industrial worker, man has usurped her field almost entirely (the needs of her family drove her to the manual arts, while her companion man hunted and fought. The former clings to him still in spots, the latter he has carried through all the centuries until we find its climax in the present world struggle).

If you turn to the Fourth Chapter of Genesis, you will find that reference is made to two women — Adah and Zillah. Adah, mother of the first man to dwell in tents and his brother, who learned to handle the harp — no doubt strung by his ingenious mother. And Zillah, who had taught her son to make useful articles in brass and iron, things needed in tent life. No doubt, these boys, preferring to stay home and help, were dubbed "Sissy and Milksop" by their comrades (if that early language could embody this idea, and I have no doubt it could) for choosing the homely occupations rather than the fighting. While man has always professed to adore woman, he has ever considered it part of the indication of developing manhood to decry her. So her struggle upward through the ages has been one long (but surely winning) battle for recognition.

Man has valued woman only for her sex value, and cared little or nothing for her industrial value.

A man's mistress is better paid than his stenographer, or woman clerk, and often better treated than his wife.

The conception of woman has been based on an old couplet too often!

> "Oh! woman in our house of ease,
> Uncertain, coy and hard to please,
> When pain and anguish wring the brow,
> A ministering angel thou."

As a child I adored these lines. I thought I saw plainly why we poor women needed a strong man to cling to. To me it was beautiful

---

[4] Constance Lynd, "Women's Independence for the Sake of the Race: Woman Must Become as Economically Independent as Man," *Woman's Century*, October, 1919, p.16.

to be so wobbly; here lay the idea of the vine and the tree, with which I was all too familiar. When grown to years of maturity I wondered what it meant. I know now. Every woman was not thus designated. It was woman's nineteenth century label, pasted on her in capital letters by her brother man.

Do you know why we were thus designated? Did you ever try to put a cork into an effervescing bottle? If not, try it, and see how it works. That is exactly what has happened, and scientific man could not decipher it. Womanhood has begun to effervesce. Because every woman did not take any man who offered her a home and board, and because some did not take to home and house work, as all her line of feminine ancestors had done, and was reaching out for the forbidden fruit of freedom in thought, education and industry, someone wrote those touching lines.

It was the yeast of the evolution of the race, and it is a mighty hard job to control it. Woman entered industrial life with a handicap. Girls taught for the magnificent sum of two hundred dollars a year, while her favoured brother got for his initial salary five and six hundred dollars, and that in Old Ontario — the girl having the same qualifications, working the same hours and frequently better work being done than by the man.

Why? Female labour was cheap (not because of her unfitness to perform it, or lack of training); it was cheap just as slave labour is cheap. The woman is not considered as belonging to herself. She is "out of her sphere," and to keep her in her sphere, we must keep her down financially, so she will do her God-given work, or the race will suffer, was man's idea.

I remember hearing Dr. Adam Shortt descant for nearly two hours before a Woman's Canadian Club as to the reasons "Why women must never receive equal pay for equal work."[5] It did not appeal to the thinking woman, for she knew the trend of the age. In future,

---

[5] This was Dr. Adam Shortt (? - 1931), a noted academic and civil servant in Ottawa at this time. Shortt was married to Dr. Elizabeth Smith Shortt, who was then one of the three women to achieve a PhD from a Canadian university. Elizabeth Smith Shortt was also first Convener of Public Health and Mental Hygiene for the National Council of Women of Canada. She was instrumental in convening a committee to petition the Ontario Provincial Government to establish Mothers' Allowances, which was achieved in 1920. What makes Dr. Adam Shortt's address so interesting, therefore, is the fact that it was clearly unacceptable to the Calgary Women's Canadian Club.

all woman's work must be paid for at a rate based on the quality and quantity of the work done, not on her sex. That day has gone.

Two million women were employed in England prior to the war and there are thousands and thousands more now.

Woman has no more right to be idle than man. Idleness breeds vice in either sex. Every one has his or her contribution to make to the world's progress. I know full well that the Madonna (the picture of the woman with the child on her breast) fills the mind of most people, and I realize the full meaning of the picture. Still, it is pure sentiment to try to bring all women at all times of their lives into accord with that picture. As if it represented the only aspect of the grown woman! What of the years preceding and the years following the growth of her family? These years belong to the State. "That the race may rise, woman must die to the old idea of her destiny, to rise a new woman." For the sake of the race she must be free to labour, free to love, free to work out her own ideas in life as a person.

The race of the past has been dominated by the male. Milton has put it thus:

> "He for his God
> She for the God in him"

and sometimes she could not find it even with a high power telescope.

I would write it thus:

> "He is for his God,
> And she for her God,
> And neither will worship the same,
> But twixt them twain, they may and will
> Frame up a true God."

Woman must be free to choose her work and pursue it, for not until she undertakes motherhood freely, shall we have a race of human beings as uniformly happy, healthy and comely as God meant them to be.

Men have not hesitated to take our work. They cook and bake, they weave and spin, they sell lace and feathers, they do our hair and make our clothes, and we have not cried out, "keep them in their place" — we have no fear. Even though they have told us we cannot compete with them, "because of our lack of physical strength." Even though they left us little save the drudgery of the world. Women have been the world's drudges! "The slaves over the cooking stoves of Christendom. In the north of England, she is a pit lassie; in the south, she is an agricultural labourer. In Germany, she is still harnessed alongside a dumb beast and drags a loaded cart or plough." Such has been her lot. We will not discuss her physical ability. But one thing is true: the new rising generations of out-of-door, skating, hockey, tennis and golf-playing girls will have and do have far more strength than their mothers had.

In the home, where she is paid not at all, she works longer hours than any man and often far into the night.

There she is the cook, seamstress, nurse, laundress, housemaid, etc. In the office, she does one line of work and is paid for it, and has at least "hours off."

Woman is coming fully into industry, and the safety of man lies where the safety of woman lies, in "equal pay for equal work." Thus I say that the only way to ensure woman's undertaking her great task for the race freely, at nature's bidding rather than because of being driven to it for support, is to make her economically independent.

Someone has said we would alter the old lines:

> "For men must work,
> And women must weep."

Thus:

> "For men must work,
> And women must work too, or
> Else there will be cause for weeping."

We are weeping (both of us today) over life's evils, induced by this very disparity of sex in industry.

"BORN A MAN, DIED A SENATOR"[6]

Recently a great deal has been said and written regarding this august body. Personally we object to some of the remarks that have been made. When Grandma is old — be kind to her — deal with her gently. Some of the remarks have been absolutely rude.

But what is the use of paying some ninety men the sum of $2,500 each, annually? Men who too often have their position

---

[6] Constance Lynd, "Shall We Abolish the Senate?" *Woman's Century*, December, 1919, p. 55.

through "political pull," or as a gift, for services rendered to a party, or as a sort of "pap" to the man, who in a constituency has done the "underground" work of the party, yet who has never been successful in winning an election. "Verily they have their reward."

As women, have we any reason to especially desire this body? We say frankly No! When Samantha Allen was sent as a delegate, for the first time, to a great convention, her husband (amused at the novel situation) said: "Well, Samantha, what good will you be at a convention; you never was at one before.[7] What can you do?" Her reply was, "Well, Josiah, I can object."

Many today are asking the question, what good are the Senators? My reply is, "They can object."

In the recent desired legislation regarding the protection of girlhood from moral vampires, the women of Ontario asked that the age of consent be raised to 18 years. It was agreed in the House, but the Senate objected.

Some years ago, the women of a western city went to a certain Senator and asked for his signature to a petition requiring that a man could not will away his property and leave his wife penniless (as many were doing), because there was no law to prevent [it].

He (the Senator) "objected," true to his calling, "because it would hamper business, if a dower law were in vogue." That act prevented a dower law for that province for at least ten years. He's still being paid for "objecting."

As women, we have no right or reason for loving the Senate. So what we don't love we'll just get rid of, and clear the decks for action.

Many a good man has been spoiled by becoming a Senator. "Born a man, died a Senator," might be a fitting epitaph on many a Senator's tombstone.

We have reached a period of reconstruction; let us do it in earnest and have a real genuine house-cleaning, the kind we used to have before the days of vacuums and no carpets. The kind we used to have, when we kneeled all day, screwdriver in hand, picking up tacks, to loose the carpet and get it out on the line, and then the beating of it! Hard work? Of course it was, but then the joy when

---

[7] Samantha Allen was the pseudonym for the popular writer Marietta Holley (1836-1926). Holley was born in Jefferson County, New York, and lived out her life in the area. As Samantha Allen she addressed the inequality of women, their lack of legal rights, their marginalization within the church, and the social assumptions surrounding their roles in life.

it was all over. Judging by press reports, there has been some carpet lifting in the political rooms of Ontario.

Someone referred to the Senate as a body of "old women." Why not have the real "old woman," with a woman's heart, and a woman's outlook, and a woman's care for girlhood, wifehood and motherhood? If we must have a Senate, let it be composed of at least one-half women (real ones). Why not? Should we succeed in our endeavour, the Senate will dissolve in a twinkling. Women on the Senate! Oh, ye gods! What is Canada coming to? They'd come in handy to push the "perambulators" of the aged and infirm members, those unable to walk, as depicted in a recent article of *MacLean's* on the same subject.

Of all the positions in the Canadian Government, I'd love to be a Senator. They look so wise, so sleek and well cared for. Why, the very name Senator proclaims what he of course is. Candidly the Senate once had a real use. Now it is looking round for uses, to justify its being. Let us pick up the tacks, get it on the line, and beat it until, like any old carpet, it goes to pieces, and the country is ready for some new regime.

"A MINISTER OF MATERNITY"[8]

Today, the civilized world, stunned by the war, is at last realizing that the best of her stock, for perpetuating the race, has been slaughtered at the front. At home are remaining the unfit, the men also who have not the stamina in them to face the enemy (we speak not of those, who through force of circumstances, have remained at home), and the slackers, to perpetuate the race. What will be the result?

The foreigners in our midst have usually large families of from ten to fourteen or eighteen children, owing to early marriages. Our Anglo-Saxon girls usually spend from three to six years longer at school than the foreign girls.

After the war, these nations who have fought with us the battle for freedom will come to our shores, and anyone can see it will only be a few years until we Anglo-Saxons will be outnumbered by the children of the foreign people.

What is to be done? This is a matter of vital interest to our life as a nation. If we are to preserve our Canadian ideals, we must have children to perpetuate them. There has been much talk that "to increase population, we would have to allow plurality of

---

[8] Constance Lynd, "Race Suicide," *Woman's Century*, February, 1920, p. 49.

wives." We do not need more population, gotten in any sort of way, but we need better population and more of it. The harem idea as suggested above does not in any way appeal to the women of this century. We know there are men who would gladly travel backward; but woman's face is set toward the rising, not the setting, of the sun, and such an idea to them is utterly abhorrent.

But population we must have — why not a minister (a woman) of maternity? The words ... are the unexpressed feelings of hundreds of thousands of our English speaking race today. "I will not be responsible for bringing into this world children who will have to suffer and struggle as we have," and can you blame them? The average Anglo-Saxon wants education, refinement, beauty and comfort in his surroundings. The day is past when poverty is a virtue, and an acknowledged aid to righteousness. It is a false idea. Poverty is no greater adjunct to character building than riches. It needs an equally strong person to stand the extreme of either. There are too many people who read "Blessed are the poor in spirit, for theirs is the kingdom of heaven," thus, "Blessed are the poor, for they shall inherit the kingdom of heaven," and then proceed to deal with the men and women accordingly. The factory owner, the storekeeper cut their employees' wages as low as possible, and as the capitalist's pockets swell with the cash he accumulates, his heart swells likewise, over the thought of what a service he is doing to these people; why, if he'll only keep them poor enough, the "kingdom of heaven" is theirs.

Then they tell us the greatest Man of history was a poor man. Yes, poor in the sense of no riches. But he was "a carpenter's son," and a carpenter can usually earn a good living. He was educated and refined. He visited the best homes and wore the best garment of his day, the seamless robe.

It is not fear on the part of womanhood today that is keeping the families small. The heart of woman is as sound today as it ever was, but too many of us have come up through the struggle and strain to want to be responsible for others having the same. Every mother, as she looks at her firstborn babe, has visions of its future. She sees him growing up in all his youth and strength, and she desires to see him something better than father and mother have been. How many thousands of mothers, when they have found that father cannot produce enough for the common necessities of life, and when the doctor's bill has been paid for bringing her little one into the world, finds she has nothing with which to provide for the actual needs for her child, has said with aching heart,

"There can be no more children here." "It is a crime to bring children into the world thus."

Then again there is the little family, so comfortable but father is taken sick, perhaps he dies or is no longer able to work; mother is delicate, poverty enters (and I am now thinking of a family in our city, only one of many). Poverty comes in, that angel of blessedness that leads men "right to heaven."

The prophet said, "give me neither riches nor poverty," but he wanted enough, and that is what God intended every man and woman to have that comes into this world.

"How can this be done?" I hear some one say. You forget that Christ said, "the poor ye have always with you." That was the present tense. He did not say "shall have." He knew the time would come when we would not have them, and it will, as surely as the sun rises and sets.

How will it come? The state says, "the child is its greatest asset." Then it is time the state opened its eyes and saw that it must take care of its greatest asset. No businessman would do otherwise.

How shall it be done? By the state mothering them. Give us mothers' pensions. Give us children's pensions. Free the mother and child from poverty.

Let the state assure every mother that the children brought into her home shall be clothed, fed and educated.

Take away the worry and anxiety from the mother's heart, and see what happens to the race. If we can give the mother and child help in the midst of all our enormous expenses in equipping men for the front and for shot and shell, can the state not do as much for the "brave little soldier" who goes into a battlefield and faces death without a murmur, that men may live, and that a child may be born into the world and add one more to the state's greatest asset.

Can we not have a minister of maternity in Canada (a woman)? Can we not lead the way in this? Then when our women know that the state will care for, educate, and clothe her child if she cannot, and give it an equal start in life, mothers will not hesitate to bring children into the world. Look into the faces of many a mother whom you meet on the street, and read the whole story of disappointed, weary, exhausted motherhood for whom the state has little consideration, but when the state wants her children to protect the state in times of war, she puts her hand on them and asks (and sometimes compels) them to go and fight for her. Ask many, whose lives have been one long struggle for existence from babyhood up, to lay down their lives for that state, which has done little or noting to alleviate their misery, or give them a fair chance in life.

The motherhood of the future must be lifted to a height never yet attained. The state must recognize her value by protecting her in her hour of greatest need, and then saying to her, "don't worry, the state will care for your child. You shall rear it, but the state assures you of plenty of food, clothing, a home, and education for that being, without which the state would not exist — the boy and girl."

Why not a minister of maternity? We have a minister of railways, and ministers of finance, of education, of agriculture, and ministers of fisheries, but none for the protection of the race. Surely our boys and girls are of as much value as the fish. All these officers do benefit the race, but why not a minister of maternity to care for and protect the boys and girls physically and mentally, that our race may excel.

"MARRIAGE AS A CAREER"[9]

There is not anything so vital to the human race as marriage and its results. At the same time there is nothing which is left more to haphazard. That which should be carefully thought out and considered is undertaken thoughtlessly and with no care, depending on the idea prevailing in the stories of the past, ending always with the fairy tale which reads: "and so they were married and lived happily ever after."

Love alone is not sufficient to make a happy marriage. Marriage per se does not make heaven, but often it makes hell; not because it is marriage, but because a good thing for the race and state is undertaken in a wrong way. The young woman (I speak of her personally), because in a sense marriage effects a more radical change in her life than the man who enters it. She must consider leaving one occupation to enter another. The war has brought many changes in our social and industrial life, but none is greater than the revolution as to the position of woman. She has served in every capacity, from maker of munitions to gardener, and made good. It is therefore necessary that, as women, we study the question of "careers" from a viewpoint never before achieved.

From this viewpoint we must consider first, the one which is most vital to the race, yet which is usually the least considered, "that of marriage." In the past we have looked upon marriage as

---

[9] Constance Lynd, "Should Marriage Be Considered A Career?" *Woman's Century*, March, 1920, p. 50.

the end, when in reality it is the beginning of a "career." A "career" upon which girls enter, from all classes, without any training or preparation, save love.

Somehow the knowledge of housekeeping, hygiene, sanitation, care of children, pre-natal influences, are supposed to be miraculously given at the marriage altar.

Could we gain the viewpoint of marriage as a "career," and were women given training for it, we would not find intelligent and educated girls looking upon it as a refuge for women "destitute of brains and ambition, and a regrettable interruption in an otherwise brilliant career of a trained woman."

These women who have heard their country's call, and have done so nobly in war, we look to them to strive for, and attain a higher ideal of marriage.

The idea of the "protecting husband" and "submissive wife," or the "Oak and the Vine," has gone forever, but the idea of two together seeking to carve out a "career" greater than either would have alone, must prevail.

But, says someone, "a woman's work in the house is drudgery, one is so tied by it, no freedom or liberty." Did you ever hear anyone pity the woman doctor, lawyer, missionary, artist, musician, teacher, stenographer, banker, because her days were so filled with work, and she was so "tied by it?" Any work undertaken is a "career," and to make a success of it is trying. But what greater work could any woman have than that of bringing into this world four or five healthy, active, clear brained boys and girls. To watch their growth and development, and to train them again in ideals for their "career."

There may be monotony in any of the above named callings, but marriage embodies so much that there is absolutely no excuse of drudgery. The girl undertaking this "career," let us see her line: companion, house director, dietitian, baby welfare, nurse, teacher, dressmaker, psychologist, law, commerce, labour, head of the CGIT and boy scouts, in fact, anything that touches life. Monotony? Never! Dull? Never! If she keeps before her the vision of her opportunity.

Such a life as this may sometimes exhaust the mind and body, but it cannot be narrowing if she gets the right idea of life. True, the girl that sees only sew and mend, cook and wash, and iron and sweep in the cycle of marriage, sees no more than the girl who stands on the threshold of life [and] asks, "Where can I make the most money?"

Today, we hope the money viewpoint of life work has gone forever, utterly toppled into oblivion by the greater word of "service."

If the new idea of the world is to pervade, viz.: service, then what greater service for her country can she do than to grasp such a career as marriage as the greatest opportunity for service, and forgetting the petty round of the daily tasks in the higher and nobler idea of service to her country. With such an idea in view, she will not want to relegate her duties almost entirely to others, while she engages in a social or club career, and now, mayhap a political career. She will not talk of "penalizing motherhood," because she must give up to a certain extent these things during the growing years of her family, but will learn from them and gain from them the ideas (while she serves and waits) that will send her forth to be a tower of strength to the mothers of the next generation.

Let our girls get rid of the idea of children as "encumbrances," and see in them the opportunity for the greatest service given to woman. Then marriage will cease to be a refuge, and become a "career" in earnest. We will then have better fathers and mothers, and homes and children, and the love stories to be written in the years to come will read: "She chose marriage as her career, and success crowned her efforts," which will mean much more than the old adage of "lived happily ever after."

Happiness is not necessarily achievement. The clam is happy (if we may ascribe this quality to such an inert mass), so too, is the bird, but who would choose the former [over] the latter. The bird has at least served.

"IT WAS A MAN WHO FOUNDED HAREMS"[10]

Two things set us thinking on this line. One, the article in the April *Century* entitled, "Birth Control," in which the author distinctly laid down the law that the only "legitimate" birth control was the control of the parents, of their own bodies, and primitive passions. To all of which we say Amen.

The second thing was an address delivered in the West by a prominent social worker, a man, who made a scathing indictment of woman, her dress, etc., as a temptation to men. He told how they should dress — so as not to "tempt" men. Suggested the idea of coddling them.

---

[10] Constance Lynd, "Men — Women — Dress — Morals," *Woman's Century*, June, 1920, p.10.

If man is the stronger sex, then it is time he got out of his swaddling clothes and became what he professes to be — the protector of womanhood, not its destroyer.

We will deal with the subject under five heads:

1. Men and women.
2. Men and women's dress.
3. Women and men's dress.
4. Men and morals.
5. Women and morals.

Men and Women. One the counterpart of the other, made by the same God, ordained to the same work, viz: the subjugation of the world into which they had been projected, and with that, the subjugation of their own bodies — mentally, morally and physically.

Endowed with the same frailties, given the same desires and passions, tempted and tried, equally with man, woman has made a greater success of subduing her physical nature than he.

The very thing that man insisted on in woman — virtue — has been her making.

The fact that man told woman "he was different," and that the seventh commandment was not a masculine command, and she believed it has been the undoing of man.

Once in the dim aeons of the past the male existed only to fertilize the female — and died. Later, he became endowed with a brain and a soul — the captain and compass of his body. But they have not ruled, nor has he sought to rule this part of his nature, in general.

Young lads, in their teens, get their minds filled by filthy and suggestive stories, often told by older, and professedly decent men, in their hearing.

Recently the dean of a boys' school asked the head of a ladies' school the following: "I do not know much about girls, but do girls when on their own corridors do a lot of nasty talking?" She replied: "No, once in a while you'll find such a girl, but she is usually shunned by the other girls. The fact is, she is looked on as degenerate, and is dismissed quietly."

Just here is where the whole trouble begins. Until fathers are as insistent as mothers regarding the clean-mindedness of their boys, as the mothers are of their girls, we shall fail utterly in producing a clean race — for "as a man thinketh in his heart, so is he."

It's the race — the next generation — we are concerned about, and you cannot have a clean race with one of its sources unclean.

Men and Women's Dress. From the dawn of creation, man has decked himself out to please himself. He then reached out and began to dictate the dress for woman. Man today dictates our fashions, and then persecutes us for adopting them.

We are not sure that Mother Eve's first covering was not designed by her other half; at least there is no data to disprove it.

Man began the harem idea — keeping the women's faces veiled, lest a man looking on their fair features should be tempted to evil.

We have grown away from the idea of woman as a temptress, though there are nations which still cling to man's (we mean the male sex's) depravity and seclude and cover their women from the vulgar gaze.

At the time of our arrival on this mundane sphere, the chief part of our anatomy, which must be covered, as being upsetting to man, was legs. Just why we've never been able to fathom. We have gotten away from that. The YWCA swimming pool, the school gymnasium, the school and college ball and tennis field, have all and each played their part in abolishing the awful evil of female legs. Today, a woman wears a skirt so short that in her mother's day it would have branded her as a loose woman.

Man are now used to the female extremity, and not a shy wink or peep is observed, as my lady trips gaily across the street, as unencumbered by skirts as her brother. Or she may ascend the steps of a street car, exposing her silken hose to the knee, and no longer is she the subject of coarse jest, or even a suggested temptation. We are facing another grave danger. Today, women are covering their ears in the style of hair-dressing prevalent among girls. A day is coming when dame fashion will decree the uncovering of these appendages and we'll hear the cry from the male portion of the race — "How immodest!"

A number of ladies who had listened to a regular tirade against the thin waist (of any description) by a male lecturer, were discussing the subject in a heated debate. All were indignant, when one said, "All I have to say is, let me clean up their dirty minds." This is true. Invariably when such tirades are indulged in, by public speakers of that sex towards habits, dress, etc. of women, look out for past history of the same.

Women and Men's Dress. Being a woman, I can only give a woman's viewpoint.

Did men ever hear us complain of "our temptation" because they wore tight suits and exposed the masculine form?

They may turn down their shirts, playing tennis or golf, and expose their hairy chests, but women never complain, or raise an S.O.S. signal, never even discuss their appearance. They may go swimming with only trunks. They may appear on the ball field or lacrosse field with little more than the proverbial fig leaf, still the women never raise a cry of "temptation!"

There must be some reason back of the two standpoints. What is it? Simply this — woman's mind (from the sex standpoint) is more wholesome than man's. What a man cultivates, woman seeks to subdue.

Men and Morals. The question is often asked, "Are the moral standards of man as high as woman's?" Personally we say no, only theoretically. Everything has combined to make them lower.

Man has always insisted on a higher moral standard for woman than for man. Social customs prove it — our unequal laws prove it.

A man will make friends of a man whose moral records are black as ink. At least he used to. There are signs of a decided change for the better today, and our best men are asking clean men for friends, and a "white life for two."

In a recent police court trial, a man of good standing in the community was mixed up with two horribly low type girls. His wife was on a visit east. He could have gone on twenty visits and his wife would never have been mixed up with two or even one degenerate or any other kind of a man.

When a specialist on this subject was talking recently, he said, "Men will co-habit with any kind of a degenerate" (and, by the way, 97 percent of all girls so inclined come under the head of mentally deficient) "but it is said to the everlasting credit of woman, she will have nothing to do with a degenerate man."

Woman and Morals. Are women's morals higher in standard than man's? We say yes, most emphatically. Man may believe in as high a standard, but he does not put it into practice as woman does.

If woman's moral ideals are higher, then there must be a reason. Let us look backward to get our viewpoint.

It was David who killed Bathsheba's husband that he might have her. It was his son Solomon who had seven hundred wives and three hundred concubines. It was a man who founded harems. No woman ever kept a male harem (only as perhaps we might apply it to commercialized vice today) and yet those poor souls, selling their souls for the mighty dollar, losing their health in five or six years, and an unhonoured grave, do this only because back of them someone sinned and left them with a mental development too weak to cope with the enticements of man.

Isn't it about time men let us alone and turned their attention to cleaning up their own backyards?

Man, who should be first to protect his offspring from disease and evil surrounding, has been last to measure up. Women have been in the forefront of the battle for a "white life for two." It took a war to make man understand that "the wages of sin is death" and bestir himself and think. Let man control his sex functions. Let him be just what we call commonly *decent* and the race will be a long way on the road to perfection.

It is a significant fact that at the weekday luncheons of the Rotary Clubs no one may tell a suggestive story. Whoever heard of women needing a prohibitory law of this kind at their club functions?

Women of Canada! There is a penalty we pay when we step over God's law. Men will need a penalty to act as a deterrent to sin; that penalty must be a heavy prison sentence for adultery. Adultery must be made a crime.

"Constance Lynd has always a refreshing and original way with such a subject as this one. She makes it clearly understood that she knows that there are many men who view these questions from the high ideals which women would like to see, but she is courageous enough to point out that men have laboured under a bad standard set in the past while, by the very force of circumstances, women have had a better standard imposed upon them. This gives, of course, all the greater responsibility to women, though it does not exonerate men from responsibility, and it places upon both sexes the need for the purification of all standards." — Editors of Woman's Century.

"NO JURY OF WOMEN"[11]

Here is something in which woman has made little progress, and one on which she must insist until accomplished.

I don't know why she has made so little headway, save that man has told her, he was more than her equal — or peer — a sort of peer-est.

British law demands that every person has a right to be tried before a jury of peers.

In my youthful days, I thought peers meant sort of immaculate gods. Later on I found it just meant men, and now I know it does not always mean men. Peers mean equals.

---

[11] Constance Lynd, "Woman Jurors," *Woman's Century*, December, 1920, p.16.

Heretofore all juries have been composed of men, because women were not persons, therefore no peers, and were tried by the law appointed and usual jury of men.

Now a woman is a person. As such she has the right to demand a judgment by her peers. Men are not the peers of women. They cannot enter into the motives and causes that tempt women to do wrong, or yet can they understand (in many cases) her attitude of mind and soul, when wrongfully used, especially on this sex evil. Therefore she must have those who can — her equals or peers — which are and must be women.

To illustrate what I mean, some years ago in Toronto, a young married woman was being forced by her husband to enter a house of prostitution, to make money for him.

She rebelled. He continued his threats if she would not consent. In her desperation, she killed him with an axe. She was about to become a mother. The case was tried before her "supposedly" peers. The verdict rendered was:

"She should live till after the birth of her child, and then hang by the neck until dead" (and this in Christian Canada!).

No jury of women would ever have rendered such a verdict. Only women can realize what being forced into a life of shame could mean.

Womanhood rose in its power and strength all over this Dominion and said, "This cannot be" — and the sentence was changed to life imprisonment. The question is, should she have been sent to prison? She killed the man who sought to put her in one prison, only to reach another. Men do not know what a life of prostitution means to a pure woman. They never can, they never will.

Recently we have had another similar judgment.

It's time we wakened up to the need of the hour, woman's need, that justice may be done.

Let every council of women in the Dominion take this up, and face our legislators with such a plea for justice, that ere another annual comes around, we shall occupy our lawful places in this regard.

I think I hear some thoughtless woman say — "Well, I'm not going to bother, it won't affect me. I never want to sit on a jury. I don't want to be responsible for a life, or death sentence." Wait, my heedless one, by neglecting to take up the subject and see that the laws of the "peers" is enforced, you are already allowing death sentences to be passed where none should be.

Or I hear some one say, "Well, the women changed the sentence of one woman by their demand, when they felt the sentence an unjust one, why not leave it so? What we have done, we can do again."

101

We dare take no chances. Justice is better than sympathy, and right than a multitude of petitions.

Our law says — "peers" — and men are not women's "peers."

A NEW WORLD OF WORK[12]

This is the question asked again and again by thinking women. Men plan their world as they have planned their heaven, on the basis of what they want, without regard to the other half of the race and just as much a part of it as they are.

In this "new earth" we have heard so much about, with its four hour day of employment, it has never once occurred to the progenitors of the scheme to take into consideration the place of woman in it, and certainly one very large — the largest portion of workers. We have been promised, "No place in the program for hard work or thrift," and all the government money they want, without interest. Of course this means the men; no political party would ever become so gracious to women.

At the present moment people are thinking only of the unemployed men in labour, industry, office or store.

These comprise only a small portion of those who will, must, and are entitled to the same freedom from toil as those above mentioned. It must be applied to all classes and conditions of men, from the doctor who is performing an operation, and not yet completed when the clock strikes the fourth hour of toil, right down to the humble person engaged in any work which is essential for mankind's health, comfort and advancement; for we sincerely hope the new era is not to stultify mankind.

It must include women, in every walk of life, especially those who have never had any consideration as to hours of work; the wife and mother in the home, hers has always been a twenty-four hour task. And the tragedy of it all is that, "No one has ever yet collectively" cared for her soul, much less her body, in respect to hour of toil.

Womanhood today has become articulate, and is unafraid to express opinions of age-old standing.

No longer do we find her willing to be man's slave, nor yet to give forth "my husband says so." She utters her own thoughts. She too must have the hours of leisure her brother man is promised.

---

[12] PAA, 75.387 (UCCA-AC), Box 9601/1/140a, Item 6027, Constance Lynd, "A Man's World? And a Man's Heaven or Do Women Really Count?" c. 1920.

The four hour day must pertain to the woman in the store, office, factory, and home, as well.

Then to that abused woman in the home must come a like reprieve. She who has been the burden bearer from time's beginning; she has been the burden bearer, not only of the work, as well as the further burden of sustaining the race, with all its added duties.

What do we mean? Just what any mother in the home will aver: hers is a twenty-four hour duty, no absolute freedom from the care and thought of all the inmates — except in the comparatively few cases where competent help is kept.

Nominally, she begins work at 7 a.m. and is on floor-duty until 10. Added to this, if any one is sick, it is she who must be on duty to care for the afflicted one. She is expected to be up as usual, for the next day's duty, smiling and cheerful and bright, thankful for the lot which has been hers, and for what salary? Usually for board, room and clothes.

The President of the Woman's Liberal Clubs of Canada has sent forth the message that women in the home shall and must share in the four hour day.

This is what will happen:

She will begin her hours of toil at 7 a.m., and work until 11 a.m. Who is to do the work from 11 a.m. to 1 p.m. — from 3 p.m. to 7 p.m? And last but not least, the whole night shift if illness calls?

Women have no right to be discriminated against, and be compelled to toil longer than men — providing four hours of work will do the world's work per day — which I am bound to say it will not.

Women will not work in this new world, which one man described as "heaven on earth in the next ten years." We are not ready to accept the man's ideas of heaven, judging from the heavens he has created in the past, for men have created all the ideas of that other sphere.

It is so easy to intrigue men into the symbolic paradises of the past — the paradise of no work, yet never a feminine paradise in them all. We find "Happy hunting grounds," but no "Happy nursing grounds" where children may be cared for. We find no seductively moustached he-houris eternally gallant and devotedly beckoning to pious lady Moslems.[13]

---

[13] This term is rooted in Islamic scripture and means "beautiful virgins." It is derived from two Qur'anic references: Sura 44:51-55, "Yes ... and We shall wed them to dark-eye houris," and Sura 52:17-20, "They [Moslem men] shall recline on couches ranged in rows. To dark-eyed houris (virgins) we shall wed them...." Here, Emily has simply reversed the roles.

It is the man Mormon who soars to divinity; women only in indefinite numbers may also soar, if properly married to him.

Mrs. Gillman in one of her books says, "the Christian heaven is as appealing, and more so than any other to women. But no man can ever rush to death in battle stimulated by the hope of a harp, as a houris."

Consequently, we are very chary of this male Paradise which is envisioned today. So we ask what of the woman in the Home in "this heaven on earth"? Past experiences have made us leery. One man said with a joyous glint in his eye, when asked this question, "Why we'll be able to each have four wives."

Allowed, yet this still leaves a gap of many hours. A day in this "heaven" let us see. Wife Number 1 has done her stunt at 11 a.m. and is off until the next morning. Number 2, finished, has gone to bridge. Number 3, to spend the night with her mother; while Number 4 left for the theatre, and a dance and supper after, from which only the crow will know when she will return. There remains still eight hours of duty!

"IF THE SUN IS TO BLAME, DON'T BLAME US"[14]

Will you allow me, a woman (not one who ever wears evening dress, in the extreme sense, or skirts to her knees, or yet "immodest waists" but just a plain mother of boys and girls, who taught them everything they should know of their physical nature, from the time they were old enough to begin to fathom the mysteries of nature [to comment]? I realize the menace of immorality as much as any one, but I do not agree with the article referred to in your paper.[15]

First, I grant all you say in regard to the "Slaves of Fashion," but you must not forget these women are a type who would [be] the slaves of something any way. Comparatively, they are few in number.

Slavery is an old, old habit of woman's, and don't forget that man had a good big share in making her a slave. Nor has he quit it yet. Talk with the average man today, and you will find my words verified. So I say, slavery is a habit that will take years to break. Any habit is hard to change, be it good or bad.

---

[14] PAA, 75.387 (UCCA-AC), Box 9601/140a, Item 6027, Constance Lynd, "A Woman's Ideas of the Prevailing Dress and Men's Morals (Suggested by reading a synopsis of "The Menace of Immorality" in *Light*, May and June), c. 1920.

[15] This article was not available.

The writer says, "there is no quarrel with woman's desires to make herself as a attractive and beautiful as possible." Then he advises us to read First Peter 3: 3-4, viz., "Whose adornment, let it not be the outward adorning of plaiting of the hair," etc.

There is no use of quoting this passage in this stage of the game of life. It may have had the desired effect in the age in which it was written. Women know now that the men, in general from the preacher down, would prefer to walk down [the] street with a stylish woman, whose hair was tastefully arranged, and even a few ornaments of gold would not be objectionable. It rather adds prestige to the man to walk beside her.

Then he suggests that "Let her adornment be that of a meek and quiet spirit." Men have always laid great stress on meekness for women, but were we to appear on the street with only this for a covering, what a hue and cry there would be.

When Peter expressed his opinion of the proper qualities of woman, he did so in the day he lived, and there may have been a reason for it. He was a Jew with all the Jewish ideas of a woman's place in life. Had he been living today, he surely would never have said it in view of what woman has suffered in consequence. Woman cannot be meek, any more than man, out in the world of business as she is today. The fact is, she has been "meek" too long and endured the exploiting of her sex. She has her freedom today, and we must not be surprised if there is some confusion and distress. We are living through one of the greatest upheavals of time, and do not know it, at least the men do not, but we women do, and [the men] may as well get to work adjusting [themselves]. I refer to the adjusting of the sexes in their new relationship, that of "equality and self-expression," and when it has all come about (as it will in time) man himself will be the most benefitted by the dawning of the new day that is being born.

The next paragraph is headed "the Evolution of the Bustle." Had the writer headed this paragraph "The Evolution of Woman's Dress," he would have been nearer the right idea.

Why spend time on describing the evolution of the bustle (and I lived in those days, "so speak with authority and not as scribe")? In those days, the crinoline, the Grecian Bend or the bustle caused quite as much ridicule as the short skirt of today. This was the line up of talk in that day. "The frou frou of skirts and the mysteries of woman's toilet have an evil effect on the minds of men, why can they not dress differently?" and [it] was quite as much a theme of pulpit and press comment as the dress of the present time.

The writer of the article to which I refer then says this, "the short skirt greatly gratified male curiosity." This is positive proof that he was well pleased at the abolishing of the frou frou of skirts, thus giving him a chance to be moral. Candidly, I think the short skirt has been of the greatest benefit to men, and it surely has to women. In the days of the trailing skirts, should we by an inadvertent move show more than the tips of our toes, the men nearly had convulsions. Why? I do not know. Legs have never been immoral to women. Watch the men now. They never take a sly peep or wink at each other as my lady trips gaily up the steps of the street car, often showing her stockings up to the knees.

Then he asks, "Why will women follow fashion?" Well, for the very same reason that men do. Our once big sleeves corresponded to the loose trousers of the men, and when Mr. Fashion said, "All change," and tight ones were in vogue, he crawled into them, even if they were uncomfortable, and it required a shoehorn to get them on. But we never made a bit of fuss about the tight trousers or the exposing of the "male form divine."

The next paragraph to which I take exception is "A clean young man's confession." He says, "I am as clean as any girl that ever lived, but mentally I am unclean." An utter IMPOSSIBILITY. Listen now, and I will quote you some scripture. "As a man thinketh in his heart so is he."

Then he says further, "I know that such splendid specimens of girlhood (as he associates with) could not have lived or thought wrongly, and I respect them, but they constitute MY moral problem." Was ever anything more absurd? When to a normally healthy stomach if food "becomes its physical problem," you look not to the food, but to the stomach to find out what is wrong with it.

The wholesome girl is never a cause of offence, the trouble is in that young man's mind, he needs exercise and probably — circumcision.

There is an old Proverb, "The fathers have eaten sour grapes, and the children's teeth are set on edge." I know that I am on dangerous ground, but might it not have been better for that young man's physical welfare had his father practiced self-control during the period of gestation. Don't blame the women for everything. We know that it is reputed, "Eve took the apple," but Adam ate it of his own accord.

Then he goes on to say "that dress is for utility and beauty." This is right, but it must be left to the one who wears it to decide what it shall be. But that any woman wears her dress "for sex

106

appeal" I deny, unless she be a demi monde. Men read this into it because of unclean minds.

Is it not rather significant that in the rules of the Rotary Club it is distinctly stated, "No one must tell even a suggestive story at their gatherings"? Why? Because decent men who started this organization knew what happened at stag banquets, etc.

Did you ever know of a woman's club to need any such prohibition?

Woman's dress was never more beautiful, sensible, than now. It is loose, does not expose the figure (except the legs). What is wrong with that?

She is natural and men seem not to like that.

Womanhood is slowly but surely evolving a dress of her own, and to her own liking. With her new freedom, and her right to think and decide matters for herself in all things pertaining to her own sex, she is going to do it without much regard to the old time notions of what men think is proper. Men made our fashions in the past. We now have women on the job.

This being the state of affairs, it behooves man to set to work and change his viewpoint, because women think they are the best judges of their own dress.

We do not interfere with men in regard to their dress; they must let us alone, and get to work on their minds.

The writer then says, "women are complaining of the Double Standard of morals," and rightly so. Now see here, the "Double Standard" is as old as the hills, or perhaps I should say humanity.

It was Solomon [who] had seven hundred wives, not Mrs. Solomon who has seven hundred husbands. Polygamy has ever been Man's (the male sex's) fundamental sin.

Man as a sex has never tried to be anything else than polygamous. Thank God, there are men clean and pure who think men have the same right to a life of self-control as the woman.

Let the fathers set themselves to work to see that the minds of [their] sons are kept as pure as the mother[s] [see] of [their] daughters. By pure I do not mean ignorance, but knowledge. Let the fathers cease to tell filthy stories in the presence of their boys.

Personally (and heaps of other women) — I am sick to death of this continual cry and fuss of men. I have listened to it for fifty years and it is getting stale. No matter how we dress we are still, and always will be, upsetting to the morals of a certain type of man, the man who has not gotten away from his primitive instincts.

And as long as he goes whining around and blaming US for all the misdeeds he will continue to be so. Adam did this (and I cannot say I ever admired his manliness or his chivalry), so I suppose they have got the habit, and as I said before, a habit IS hard to break.

The writer then says, "Oh, for the sturdiness of a true independence." My dear sir, you are getting it! There never was a time when woman could wear just what she pleases as she can at this moment.

We are slowly evolving an American dress, but it will be neither the "flowing robes of the Greeks" or the narrow obstructing dress of the "Japanese." Woman wants freedom just as much as her brother. He cast his "flowing" robes away long ago, as unfit for real use. We, like him, have forever cast into the discard those habiliments that hinder the free action of our body.

It took man ages to develop his present dress, from loincloth, robes, right through lace and velvet, with short pants that "exposed the legs," until he attained the present dress.

Women, we are told, began with "fig leaves." Evidently she always did wear fragile things, and she will. WE CANNOT STAND THE HEAVY CLOTHING OF THE MAN. What if as the writer says, "the girl of this day has not always calculated the thickness of her garments, and sometimes shows the silhouette of her form in this Western sun?" If the sun is to blame, don't blame us. I'd suggest putting blinkers on the sun (son)?

Why is it immoral to see the shadow of a form? Men surely know what we are. Just stop thinking about us and keep busy.

For the curious ones, I would suggest a course in female sexology, under some fine Christian man who could give advice that he has followed, and let his "curiosity" be satisfied, and thus give him a chance to fling loose from this awful body of "curiosity" so that he will no longer be upset by every passing thin waist, short skirt or pair of silken hose.

NOW LISTEN ....Your prayer for a "sturdy independence" has been answered. You have it in woman's attitude toward much of the "cant," for it is nothing but cant, that men have used always to make life miserable for us, and to tyrannize over us.

WOMANHOOD is saying to you, "We know your tricks .... Get out of your swaddling clothes and be men in earnest.

Woman is thinking for herself and is evolving. She has a place in life she never had before. She is perfectly independent to live and think and act as she deems best. The fact she is doing it "is grievous in our eyes" — quotation from the Gospel of MAN, Chapter 1, verses 1001-1002.[16]

She is paying very little attention to what man thinks of her. She is not at all impressed with the past record of man, or his moral attitude toward her, even when she was all covered up bodily, yet he insisted that she be veiled to keep him from seeing even her face. Woman today has no slightest idea that she has anything to do with the upsetting of man's morals or that her dress makes any difference at all.

She's out on her own, and the sooner man turns his attention to cleaning up his inner self (as woman has done) [and] he thinks no evil, and ceases his whining, and crying about our "immoral" dress and becomes a man indeed, strong in purpose, to control his whole being — well — then we will have a different world to live in.

> Have we women always wanted what you gave to us before?
> Did we want your veils and harems, in the Oriental races?
> Did we ask to be unclean, shut out of sacred places?
> Did we beg for "scolding bridles" and "ducking stools" to come?
> And clamor for the "beating stick" no bigger than your thumb?
>
> Did we seek to be forbidden from all the trades that pay?
> Did we claim the lower wages, for a man's full work per day?
> Did we petition for the laws, wherein our shame is shown?
> That not a woman's child, nor body is her own?
> What women want has never been a strongly acting cause,
> When woman has been wronged by man, in churches, customs, laws.

---

[16] This is purely a sarcastic play on the scriptures being used as a primary source of authority. It is to demonstrate that men's ideas of what women should do are not the same as those contained with the Gospels of Jesus Christ.

"TO PRODUCE THE FINEST FRUIT, WE THIN OUT THE BLOSSOMS"[17]

During the past months, few subjects have received the attention which has been given to that of birth control.

Its various phases have been discussed, from every angle, in homes, in clubs, in all ranks of society, also the Press. The last, for the most part, expressed the viewpoint of the male section of the country.

Women of all Protestant denominations are grateful for the pronouncement of the great Lambeth Conference, which resulted in a vote of three to one of its members — refusing for the first time in history to condemn it. It was a negative vote, but it was far more; it was progress.

But the most amusing thing has occurred. Two men at different times, in different places, have delivered their *ipse dixit* on the theme — and they each are bachelors.

The one a Protestant clergyman; the other a Catholic priest.

The first question, which one is led to ask is — "What do they know about it from any concrete angle?" This is a fair inquiry, as each being a bachelor, it carries its own implication.

Apparently the time has come for woman to speak; she is the one most concerned, except the child. She has kept marvelously silent on the subject — considering her reputation for talking — and its infinite importance to the race. The innings are hers now. She'll try and make a goal.

First — the Protestant clergyman bachelor; his remarks were made at a meeting for the mothers in a Western city, called that he might instruct them regarding their duties in the home, the care of their children, and a host of other things of which he knew nothing. It is rather a delicious morsel to hear a bachelor speak on these topics. Of course, there was a time when women thought the male (especially if he were a minister) was an infallible guide in all matters; he said he was, and that settled it.

This bachelor did not know that Western women had outgrown that idea long ago; so when he ventured out on the thin ice of birth-control, expounding their duty in these words, "It is your obligation to have all the children you possibly can; it is your service to the world, your country, and your God." It was too much, something happened, the ice cracked. These ladies who had

---

[17] PAA, 75.387 (UCCA-AC), Box 181, Item 6028, Constance Lynd, "Ladies, The Bachelors, and Birth Control," c. 1925.

listened with perfect decorum until this last remark rose en masse, walked out of the church hall, indignant that a bachelor should presume to instruct them on such matters. He retired, we hope, a chastened and more intelligent man.

Bad as was his mistake, his decree was a trifle ahead of a book recently written, also by a man, perhaps a bachelor, in which he went so far as to declare that, "Women who had practiced birth-control, as well as women who might have married and did not, would be faced in the world to come by all the little lives that might have been." If this is so, there will not be many of the bachelor girls craving for that terrestrial [*sic*] realm.

Ignorant as was the Protestant bachelor's statement, he at least had the consideration to confirm woman's obligation to this mundane sphere, and not erect scarecrows for her to face in the Beyond.

It is truly perplexing to understand why men put such stress on "woman's duty" in this matter, and especially on the multiplicity of children. Will some man badly infected by this germ release the secret? Candidly, women consider it is none of their concern.

Women know all about the, "Be fruitful and multiply" of the Bible; but they know something else, which perhaps some men have not stopped to think about, namely, that twice one makes two is multiplication, equally with twice twelve is twenty-four. Think about it. It will add to your knowledge.

The Catholic priest now enters the arena, asserting the same thing, and a like obligation. He has a bogy. These mythical creatures were effective and most efficient before women became human beings or had brains with which to think. He told them in a breathless voice, how "men and women would become" — (think of it) — "bestial, sensual, and irreligious, if birth control were practiced," evidently quite unaware that it is already an established thing.

It is a delightful characteristic, this telling others their duty, but somewhere is an old proverb, "People who live in glass houses should not throw stones." What about these bachelors? They are practicing birth-control with a vengeance, not even reaching the first stage of the multiplication, also are they not labelled "bachelor." By what right have they, Protestant clergymen or Catholic priest, to say a word? The condition of this world at the present moment leaves no room for doubt that there is urgent need of widespread action, if we desire to maintain our present civilization at its highest point and advance still to greater elevations.

111

In days gone by, war was looked upon as a means of keeping down population, and ridding the world of the weak, the unfit, and the defective.

If this is true, do we realize what we make of the Creator? We attribute to him the qualities of a demon to the nth degree, cruel and unkind. Cruel to put woman through the pangs of childbirth, only to eventually cull them out, through the awful scourge of war, making our babies only cannon fodder for His next clash of arms.

Unkind to bring into such a world babies who never asked the right to be born, who must end their days on God's battlefields; torn in anguish of body — to die alone and uncared for, with the sole purpose of population reduction. If this is correct then is [warfare] the greatest instrument in the hands of the Almighty, doing His work perfectly?

Modern warfare does not rid the world of its unfit, weak and inefficient; they are useless. Only the fittest were sent to the last holocaust; the weak and unfit remained at home to propagate their kind, which they do to perfection. If care is not exercised immediately, a century hence we will be a nation of imbeciles and half-wits.

Can you imagine a young mother as she holds her firstborn son in her arms, and smiles into his face, as she croons her lullaby, a melody in which the words run like this:

> You dear little piece of cannon fodder,
> You dear little piece of cannon fodder,
> Soon, soon, you'll be perfectly fit
> To die on one of God's battlefields,
> How happy I'll be when you're hit.

Neither the rhyme, nor the rhythm, nor message is correct, but it is just as fine as the logic of the bachelors. Such does not express woman's idea of God. This is not "race progress," but heathenism of the grossest order.

Poor woman! Why cannot men mind their own business and turn their attention to their brothers, telling them their "duty." Were women to interfere with men and assert their right to tell men their duty as they do to us — My! What a storm they'd raise.

It's all a remnant of old and bygone days, which we hoped had passed forever. It is time men in general cleared the cobwebs of antiquity from their brains, and lived in this wonderful present century of advancement in knowledge, in science, in culture, forgetting the days when women were slaves, and at least tried to remember they are persons of education, and thoughtful members of the world, society, and a human being just like themselves. She is his toy no longer but an equal, and in many ways his superior.

Man's dominance of woman's kingdom is fast breaking up; God knows it needed to do so. It is only part of the evolution of the human race. Once they threatened us, burned us as witches, when they desired to get rid of us for some younger and fairer form.

… Thank God this has passed for the most part; woman's body is her own, her child is her own; it was through her efforts it has come, and she wants the very best child she can produce, the finest she can have for its development, in health, education, environment, and she'll have it, even if it means birth-control.

Woman has become articulate; with her higher education and knowledge of science and biology she has struck a new pace. The world is hers equally with man; she is the captain of her soul, the chart and compass of her own destiny. No fear of man deters her, she must think her own thoughts, and follow the gleam of the high ideals which come to her as the mother of the race. She knows she is the race, it is through her the race flows; man's part in the race production is to hers, as a mere incident.

She has had sufficient experience of life to understand its meaning, and has decided her course as to production.

When in our mental homes we have more inmates than students in our universities, it is high time to halt, think, and act. In two generations our race might easily surpass all others in health, happiness, virtue and intellect; but instead we find ourselves "the sickest animal alive, and the most foolish." We breed and inbreed everything for the sake of perfection, from dogs to roses, but never think of perfecting the race. We calmly delegate all that to God, hoping that in some miraculous way He will eradicate our crimes against the on-coming generations, but He does not do it — that is our job.

Woman once laid all the blind, crippled, defective children to "God's will," and patiently endured it as "her cross" by which she would be sanctified. That idea too has gone.

Woman has good cause to know — a father may through his sin and lust, transmit to his son that which shall live on in that child's body through life. "The father may be forgiven and live in the next world as happy, and unconcerned as a cricket," but the child who inherits the future he has bequeathed him lives on earth in bodily and mental agony.

The late war showed the people of America that a large proportion of her male population were "morons, half-wits, and quarter-wits" — the mentality of a child in a grown up man, not even fit for cannon fodder.

What are the mothers of the race doing that they should be forced to breed morons for citizens? Why should they sit quietly down waiting for man, or bachelors to clean up the stygian pool? What have the fathers done that the minds and bodies of the children are corrupted?

This birth control, which until lately, one was required to speak of with bated breath, is out at last into the open. Why? The motherhood of the race is coming into action. She has had birth control and found no ill effects, she is having it and will have — all the bachelors to the country notwithstanding. She knows what no man can tell her, and she acts.

To achieve the best for the race, she must be free — free to choose when she shall have a child; free to say no; for the willing mother brings to this word the finest type of humanity because it is a wanted child, and not a forced one.

Is it right that in this day and generation a woman of twenty-seven should be the mother of seven children in eight years, with another coming, and her health failing? Better a thousand times half that number, with health and strength to rear and care for them.

What do bachelors know of the need of birth control from the negation of it? Except as they themselves practice it. By what authority do they, the Protestant clergyman, or Catholic priest, assert their dictum? Away with it all, this dangling the body of "bestiality and duty," before the eyes of longsuffering womanhood.

We would suggest a course in botany for these bachelors. They seem not to know that every blossom on an apple tree does not become an apple. Only one in scores perhaps. Watch how they fall; and then God's winds and worms take the rest.

Turn now to the human, and here to be effective, we must of necessity speak plainly, and why not?

When conception takes place, there are simply thousands which might have been, but all save one (and rarely two) [are] eliminated, pass away and die. Are you astonished? Why this waste? Again it is God. God the architect of the human frame took care of that; while man cries out against the destroying of the one, two or three, as the case may be.

Today the Creator is trying to teach us through other ways the meaning of it all.

Surely we ought to be as sensible about the production of the child as we are with the quality of our horses, cows and hogs.

It is astounding in this day of progress, in which we are not content with anything but the best of everything, from automobiles to wheat, that men should be held by superstition and worn out creeds regarding the question of birth-control. Can they not see what is coming? It is pathetic that the church which should lead is lagging behind.

When birth control is taught to men and women, as we shall yet teach the child the functions of the body, including sex, we'll do away with the bulk of illicit relations, and have happier homes, and healthier children, in body, mind and spirit.

Recently a vote was taken in certain States as to whether birth control should be taught scientifically or not. The women of the farms declared for it. So used are they to seeing the processes of nature interfered with, on animals poultry and stock, with its great success, and it is no shock to their senses. They reason thus, if this interference with the stock produces a better horse, cow or hog, why not a better child by the same means? No reputable farmer would let a mare he respected bear her young too rapidly, how much more should he protect the woman who, at the marriage altar, he promised to love and cherish?

When we take such care to produce the best in the animals, why shall we not do the same for the child? God will not undo our errors. He gave us "Dominion" over everything. And we leave undone the most important, the Race.

There is no sin or sensuality in calmly determining the number of children you are able to support properly, and limiting them to that number, than it is for a farmer to decide the number of hogs he can keep on his farm. If there is, then the sooner we all become hogs, the better.

But look; let that farmer keep his hogs, on land too poor to support them except in a state of semi-starvation, and see how soon the State will read him the Riot Act. Not so when it comes to the child.

Do not try to inform us of that old, old story, "that God sends all the Babies." He does nothing of the kind. There are millions of them He weeps over; marred and broken before they see the light of day. Of these we fancy we hear Him say, "So these are the images you have made of me."

"Have Dominion" is the watchword. Are we leaving undone that He would most see?

The rise of humanity in life, to the perfection He has figured. Is fear keeping us from our duty?

... We have a long way to travel. This is the goal of womanhood, and God grant she shall never cease to strive for it, till the race stands on this pinnacle.

Idealistic, you say? True, but nothing great has ever come to this world without someone first [having] caught the gleam. Had not man in the ages past followed the glint of his ideas, we should still be living in caves, travelling in carts, without even having the chance to live on this marvelous continent of North America.

Already woman is seeing the dawning of this new race, with her child welfare, prenatal care, baby clinics, and with the more modern education of her child, the dark clouds of superstition are vanishing. They cannot afford to [a]wait the consent of backward thinking men who do not even "see through a glass dimly," and are bound by traditions, fables and old men's tales. Men who mayhap still think the earth is flat, that woman was made from one of our male ancestor's cast off ribs. Had they told us it was their backbone which had been utilized for the momentous event, it would in many cases be easier to believe.

The idealism of the lines quoted is already here — man is and has developed his power in earth, sea and air — as each passing year testifies. He is having dominion over that strange fire of electricity; new arts are here, and will be more and more; music divine rings through the skies; but what of the Race?

Still there are lives of little children where is no song; eyes which carry no glint of knowledge; nor are their souls aflame with God's blessing of freedom; cursed from birth, to die in shame.

If there is to be no more war, then says Dean Inge, "We shall be driven to limit our numbers in one way or another. This can best be done peaceably by birth control" and may we add sanely, humanly, and with the Godlike touch of limitation.[18]

As to the bogy of "bestiality, sensuality, and irreligion," let these bachelors read their Bibles, ready history, to find that ever since man (here we mean specifically the male) made his appearance on this globe, it is one long tale of these characteristics, from which we are just emerging. Through all past ages, woman has kept silent till now. Listen to her.

---

[18] William Ralph Inge (1860-1954) was a controversial Anglican minister from Britain. He advocated birth control and believed in eugenics. He was known as the "Gloomy Dean," due to his pessimistic views on civilization and the human race.

Womanhood of today can change the whole face of the world in two generations, if they will. Why are the nations of Europe calling for "larger families," and hastening childbirth? Is it love of the Race? Never! For they in many instances cannot support in even meager comfort the immense populations already there. It is cannon fodder, cannon fodder.

Women alone, unaided by man, can stop even the thought of more war by refusing to contribute to it the greatest necessity for conflict — namely babies. We mean control the births, or if need be, stop it altogether. Women have never really shown what they can do, nor will until they once stand together on some great issue. Don't drive them to it.

Women, let no religion's fear enter into your thought, for to secure the finest bloom of rose, dahlia or chrysanthemum, we cull the buds. To produce the finest fruit, we thin out the blossoms. Shall woman fear to do the same for the sweetest thing on earth — a little child.

Call it what you will — limiting the family to income, or better babies, or birth control, it matters not.

Had the Creator been more concerned for numbers than for the child and the mother, or the ultimate rise of humanity, He would not have limited the years of her child production as He has; else all might have been as the fabled Sarah, a story that is a biological impossibility.

The same God who put a rim round the ocean saying, "Thus far shalt thou come and no further," set a rim round the years of woman's child production, for the sake of the child, and for the sake of woman.

Women! Who shall lead us? God or the bachelors?

"THE NEW DAY FOR WOMAN"[19]

The Spirit that moved upon the deep
Is moving in the minds of men
The nations feel it in their sleep
A change has touched their dreams again.

Voices confused and faint arise
Troubling their hearts from East to West,
A doubtful light is in their eyes,
A gleam that will not let them rest.

[19] PAA, 75.387 (UCCA-AC), Box 181, Item 6028, Constance Lynd, "The New Day for Woman," c. 1930.

The dawn — the dawn is on the wing
The stir of change on every side,
Unsignalled as the approach of spring,
Invincible as the hawthorne tide.

How seldom it is given to men and women to see the dawning of a new day. Sleep closes their eyes and paralyzes the brain so that as the first rays appear above the horizon, it comes all unconsciously and unappreciated by the world at large. But day breaks. So too the dawning of the New Day for Woman came all un-noticed, until the sun was far up in meridian glory.

The dawning of this day came not with noise and commotion. No clarion call heralded its approach. It began long ago, when we shed our night-caps, hooped-skirts and quilted petticoats, and gradually donned the less durable, but beautiful garments of today.

With these, vanished also the good old "two-ply" homemade woollen stockings, and ushered in the day of silken hose. Darning disappeared with the advent of the "hole-proof," and womanhood no longer spends weary hours mending tears.

She shortens her skirts because she knows there is no danger of rents. Long skirts often hide a multitude of holes.

Today, my lady "washes her week's laundry in a hand-basin and dries it on the window pane," while fifty years ago, with frills and puffs and furbalows, she sweated over the wash-tub and ironing board all day long.

With all the shadowy thinness of her garb today, who is there after all [who] will not say "it's sensible."

In days gone by physicians railed against our heavy skirts as "ruinous and detrimental to health." "Hang every garment from the shoulders" was the cry. Today, they weigh our garments and pronounce them "too light to hang anywhere."

Oh Lord! The joys of being a woman!

We never bother with the men's clothes. Why will they bother with ours?

Men today are crying for "the old-fashioned girl," the girl who thought him a god, and believed his judgments infallible. If she came, he would not walk down the main street of any city in Canada with her.

Old ideas and customs die hard. We love the past simply because we know it. The future we fear. Humanity's face is set to the future and we may as well make the best of it.

There are still men who talk of the good old days of the crinoline and the wasp waist and Grecian Bend. They still stand with strained eye, watching the distant hills for the first glimpse of its re-appearing over the hills of time. It will never come.

Just why are men languishing for these things? They do not know it, but these were the insignia of the slavery of woman.

Fancy a girl today playing basketball with a crinoline, running a race with a wasp waist, or playing tennis with a Grecian Bend. It can't be done.

We had no Annette Kellermans in the nineteenth century. She could not have existed. A girl swathed as she was then, in the cumbersome bathing suit of the day, made a better sinker than swimmer.

Men hampered women by their insistent cry of "Not modest." Those days will never return. They are dumped into the scrapheap of woman's progress. With it all, womanhood is now more nearly as [the] Creator made her than ever in her existence since Eden. True she still clings to the ancient custom of beautifying herself with paint, and occasionally brightens up the landscape with rouge. But she will get over this, as she got over the measles.

She is the same creature today in bloomers or riding breeches as in the hoop-skirt and quilted petticoat. You cannot change her — only today she is thinking.

Over the horizon came a glow. It was the sunrise for woman. Prior to this, hers had been a life of repression, but there came a day when she realized that God meant her to have some share in the world's fun and sport.

The spirit of play coming into woman's life gave her a new sense of comradeship unknown to her ancestors. The basketball field, golf and tennis, taught her to stand her ground, where her old time sister succumbed to the "powers that be."

Women knew little of play until this century. Women were "religious." The fact is they did nearly all the real religion there was. Why they were "Pauline," and what more could you want? They were keepers at home, reverenced and obeyed their husbands, kept silence in the churches.

They provided great church suppers for the men, which on occasion they enjoyed, as it was the one sole time they need not "keep silence" and do no violence to their religious scruples, or bring down on them the disapproval of the honoured male.

Woman was religious, and play or sport (for the woman) was irreligious. It was a waste of time. Home was her place. She should be satisfied with the sport of the dishpan and the corn broom.

Chasing dirt was more religious for her than chasing a ball over the green field in God's great open air. "Men only" was written here. But she learned to play.

Some years ago, when in a church equipped for athletic sports for men, the girls asked for, and were allowed one night a week to play in the recreation room, under the instruction of a man — a man mark you to teach them to play. All the pious male saints of that church went off their bases, because of the atrocity of a "man" seeing girls in gymnasium bloomers — umph! Of course, saints of this persuasion know men, I suppose you cannot blame them. These saints bucked first, and the female saints followed. They had the habit of running in the same groove, and following a lead. There is nothing so catching as sainthood. It used to be at least.

Later on, a YWCA came into the life of that city, with its swimming pool and gymnasium. Good churchmen, and women, and may I say good Christians, come and watch the exhibitions of the girls' skill in swimming — but I almost hate to tell you — they don't wear big fluffy bloomers — Sh! Sh! — just tights. And not a modern saint ever blinks a wink.

Then when woman had achieved all this she got the idea that if the world of play was hers to share the same as man, surely the world of business was hers too. She educated and fitted herself for all positions that were formerly only open to men, and she succeeded. The remainder of the century will keep men going to be apace with her.

We know all about the question of the "coming generation, and woman refusing to perform her God-given function." It's so old, it's musty. We have yet to learn that all of them should not marry. Why waste a good lawyer, doctor, nurse or business woman, in making a poor mother and housekeeper? We do not find the female portion of the race raising a row about the men who do not perform their "God-given function of fatherhood." So why all this commotion about us?

Men and women equally are first and foremost citizens and human beings, and they should serve somewhere in their land. Let them settle first where they feel they can do this best, and the motherhood and fatherhood will take care of itself.

What our country needs is not more children, but better born ones.

This century will see woman at the head of all sorts of big businesses. She is just getting her wind — then watch her.

The clocks of time struck twelve noon when she achieved her lawful position of civic equality with man. Scientists have clearly proven that there is no sex to brains. Men used to fool us on this as on other things. Her afternoon hours of this day will be spent for the protection and betterment of childhood, and the race. "She is the race," says one writer.

The dawning of the next new day will come as the clocks of time strike twelve p.m., with its old-time man and woman, in whom the spirit shall be in the ascendant, cut loose from custom, prejudice, and flesh habit. This man and woman, the complete whole, shall stand forth in the spiritual beauty of the perfect man, made in the image of God, in the new world.

And so another day shall rise, more glorious than any preceding one. Then at last the everlasting gates shall lift, and the King of Glory shall come to this earth, embodied in the form of men and women — "Made in His Likeness."

"SHALL MARRIED WOMEN WORK?"[20]

Candidly, it is her own business; she must decide where she prefers to live her life, and she only.

Before anyone can give an enlightened opinion on the subject, she must know the facts — and knowing them, be guided in their thinking.

Secondly — she must know the past historically as to the place of woman in bygone days, and then seek to improve on the past.

Many women are blaming the present depression [on] the fact of married women working and think a law to prohibit the same would bring relief. Should all the women employed out of the home resign, it would not cause even a ripple on the surface of this world-wide condition.

It is a gigantic economic situation which would no more set affairs right by married women not working than shooting a gun at the sun would put the orb of day out of commission.

It would be possible to take country after country, of every land and continent, and prove the fallibility of the argument; but such is not necessary for people of education and knowledge — or for those old enough to know the immediate past of women, let alone the remote eras. In the past, women were looked upon as

---

[20] PAA, 75.387 (UCCA-AC), Box 960/1/40a, Item 6027, One of Them, "Shall Married Women Work?" Newspaper clipping, publication unknown, c. 1931.

quite inferior to men; a woman had no brains, no ability as to judgment; her one and only safety was her instinct, so the men said, and woman was thankful for that. She had no soul — and in many cases it was thought she achieved heaven or received hell only through favour of her husband. Where he went, so too did she. They were "one" and he was the one. She was only part of his belongings.

Centuries rolled by, when in the plan of the Creator, woman awakened; she, like her first sister, desired knowledge; prior to this, she had received only the most primitive education, the "Three R's."

It is not one hundred years yet that in the States she was accorded a high school education — and in Canada, only for less then seventy-five years. Then followed her request for a university training of the mind, and only some forty-five or fifty years since her desire was granted.

Still man smiled blandly down on his mate, she had always been considered his inferior, and he was sure she was. She could equal him in the classroom, often outdistancing him, but there was one thing lacking — she was not a citizen of any country, only as attached to her father, or husband. What a predicament! In other words, she could not vote.

Again the women of the world took up the cudgels for liberty and demanded the franchise on the same basis as the men. They had earned it, and the men knew it right well.

Some, of course, frowned on it as "it would upset the political pot." Think of it! As if the pot did not need cleaning, no matter who did the scrubbing.

In the year 1915, several of the provinces were agitating for the franchise (Alberta was among the first) — and woman was declared a citizen on an equal basis with them, so far as her country was concerned. Some men feigned pleasure at her success, and deemed that now she might be able to carve out a destiny even in the world to come — all her own, and be no longer dependent on his "journey's end."

Since then, out of 600 vocations in life, women have entered all but 23 — and you tell me, women should be legislated against if they marry.

And now arises a new generation, "who know not Moses that led them out of bondage," into the land of promise — not of honey, but of liberty and equality. Today we find that some women are demanding that if one of these emancipated women should inadvertently marry, she must be compelled by act of law to throw all her achievements aside, and undertake the eternal round of bake, wash, iron, scrub and meals three times a day, whether she is fitted for it or not.

Men do not demand this of men if they marry a wealthy woman; shall we be less just than they? Women are free human beings. Women awake! and see what you are doing. This is but the thin edge of the wedge, which some men would be only too glad to drive in with a bang, right to the top, and sit on it forever.

Coincident with this comes a nicely concealed suggestion that "women had made no use of their franchise and were not getting into parliament at all scarcely, and why let them have the vote?"

True, they are not as yet; they are very young on the job, and it is to their credit they are not rushing into places before they are ready for them.

It is not the business of woman after all in the past to curtail women's work or activities, by act of legislation, but to seek to enlarge it.

Every woman has a right to her own opinion on this matter of course, but in the last analysis, the free man will choose the woman who best can do the work assigned, or is the most capable for the position, not caring whether she is married or not. The men are free — why hamper woman? She's had quite sufficient of that.

Knowing the past, we must not look backward, but forward to the time when unemployment, cycles of depression, shall be no more; for come it must as soon as mankind finds the way. But do not shackle womanhood again in any way, it will not relieve the situation.

The day will come when we shall laugh over our short-sightedness, and shout for joy that womanhood has not receded into the dim and distant past, but is free — free to live her life as she deems best, and the old shackles have not been brought out of the dungeons of the past and clamped on her body, mind and soul.

Someone has said, "No nation rises higher than its womanhood." Let us seek for Canada the highest.

"THE STERILIZATION ACT OF ALBERTA"[21]

Your issue of January contained a short article re this much discussed subject, as applied to your own country.

---

[21] PAA, 75.387 (UCCA-AC), Box 181, Item 6928, Constance Lynd, "The Sterilization Act of Alberta, Canada," c. 1931. This article was submitted to *The Times* newspaper in London but was rejected.

It may be of interest to know that the Province of Alberta has had such a law for the past three years.

The first request was brought into the Legislature of the Province by the women of Alberta.

During the years when huge numbers of immigrants were pouring into this great country, the Canadian mother noted first the prevalence of many defects in the little ones, particularly those of a physical nature.

Consulting the medical fraternity, they were told, "It was caused by too early marriage of the mothers of the land from whence they came." In other words, immature mothers.

Later followed a vast increase of mental defectives. In one family where both father and mother were defectives — and should never have passed the Immigration Officer — with three of their offspring in an institution for such, and three more at home. [Then] with the added prospect of perhaps a dozen such, the women began to think it was time to act.

Then we were faced with crimes of these lads of low mentality against mere children, one of which so aroused the women that in 1916 a resolution was sent to the Government demanding immediate legislation, viz. for sterilization.

Some men ridiculed us, while many endorsed. Sanctimonious ones, both male and female, had religious scruples — as "interfering with the works of God."

It was war time, and while we did not succeed in securing our legislation at that time, it came later. Yet the mental defectives kept up their usual record for fecundity.

Some five years ago, the Department of Health (pushed to it we believe by the crowded condition of our mental defective home in the province) again resurrected the women's request, and the law was passed.

This law lay quiescent for two years. Why? Well, we prefer not to state. Some three years ago the law was made active and since then it has gone ahead by leaps and bounds. No one ever talked of the "Marring of the masterpieces of the gods," nor of the "right of men and women to produce their kind." They are taking it quite as philosophically as the modern methods on trees, fruits, cows and other animals, to produce a finer strain of each.

As published in the Press, during the past two years, some three hundred have been sterilized, and no comment. In fact, the persons are unknown to the community.

Some by their own request, some of criminal tendencies by

compulsion, whose tendency was to repeat and repeat their coming into court for sexual matters and bringing into this old world of ours, poor, helpless little souls, whose mental endowments were not and never would be equivalent to their needs for life. These last are for the most part, court cases, by which the law permits enforced sterilization after due investigation and medical examination, by men and women so appointed for the task.

So far we hear no complaints. It is simply one of the laws of our land, by which we hope to eliminate those who never should have been born, and transform into comparatively decent citizens those who can and will make good, in so far as being made capable of earning a living, and not be either a menace or a burden on the community.

COME THE REVOLUTION [22]

MEN! . . .

Awake to a new menace. Communism, Socialism, Fascism and all the other "isms" fade into insignificance when stacked up against a newly aroused and militant feminism.

Lately we have been hearing a good deal regarding man's intention of "shoving women gently but firmly back into the home."

Womanhood the world over is quite aware of this evil intention, but let me ask you before you begin shoving, that you stop and consider carefully — understandingly — and may I say, sanely, what will happen. When woman got the right of education on a par with men, it was human progress. When she decided that she did not like housework, and the care of children, and fitted herself for business, medicine, law, etc., that also was human progress. And this world is better for what woman has achieved since her education.

The path of progress never moves backward, always forward.

When the Creator made man (I mean the twain) he said in Genesis 1, 26 and 27: "Let us make man in our image and let him have dominion over everything." So in His image made He them.

"Oh!" I hear someone say — "What are you going to do with the rib story?" I'll do with it just what I'd do if someone told me that a jeweller always had to take a wheel out of an old watch to make another new one.

---

[22] PAA, 75.387 (UCCA-AC), Box 181, Item 6028, Constance Lynn, "Man, Woman and Freedom," *The Arrow*, December 1935. *The Arrow* was an American publication.

Let us go a little farther. It was Eve, not Adam, who was looking for wisdom, and the Tree of Knowledge attracted her as she had heard it would make her wise.

Ever since that fatal day the Adams of this world have stolen her brain babies. It was woman who first made the clothing for humanity; she carded the wool, made the yarn, wove the cloth to do this, and man took all this labour without even a thank you for it, and I am quite sure he never paid her a nickel. It was she who washed the clothing, she who dried the fruits and later canned them for use for the family. It was she who made the rugs, cut the worn out garments into strips and with her own hands wove them into carpets that man might have something soft to tread upon. It was she that made the butter and the cheese, in fact, she was the basis of all the early comforts that came to mankind.

What became of all this woman's work which she did in the home? Man stole it. He built his factories to manufacture these things en masse. The cloth, the rugs, he erected his dairies to make butter and cheese. He built his great canning factories and when he had contributed all this he invited womanhood to come into them and eke out a miserable existence, often amid sordid surroundings.

They took her babies of four years and five years of age "to mind their spinning jennies or pick up the fluff off the floor under the machinery." They took our children of riper years and forced them to help earn the bread for the parents, as they were cheaper than hiring men and women and we are not rid of it yet. Man has still his sweatshops where women may earn 25 cents for making a hundred buttonholes and much more could be told of work all day for 50 cents, and all this in Christian America.

As womanhood watched all this she decided the only way to cope with this state of affairs was through education — which ages before her mother Eve had sought — and with her education, the achievement of equal status with man as a person.

We would not have you infer that all womanhood and manhood are really educated. Education takes in mind, body and soul, and this triple necessity is often, even in the male, a minus quality.

Womanhood knows all about "man's imperiousness" as Miss Luke says in a recent article. But is she right in assuming so much? I doubt it.

Man has run this world himself since the dawn of creation and in this year 1935, a pretty mess he's made of it. I do not hesitate to say that man, the male, has achieved more in the last fifty years than in all the ages previous. These fifty years represent the years of woman securing education, as well as her rightful place in the world as a person, as a citizen and [as one who] received the franchise. More has been accomplished for the good of the human race in America and for the child from babyhood to maturity than ever since the man's regime began.

Men must not forget that once in the dim ages of the past a matriarchate age pertained, remnants of which may be found in Tibet. It may come again, so beware of losing your laurels while "shoving so gently and firmly." Lately, a man marched into a lady's office and said, "you've no business here. We men are going to shove you women back into the home where you belong."

"Oh," she replied, "don't you know that a home means a husband and children and there are not enough men to go around. Besides, it really isn't done today, to have children without a husband." Silently, he walked out.

It is refreshing to hear from time to time that these gracious and courtly men are going to shove gently and firmly. Personally, I like a firm hand when supplied to somebody else's back.

Before you start shoving, take a woman's advice. Stay awake nights, and think before you act.

Do you know the women of China?

Do you know the women of India?

Do you know the women of Canada?

And the twentieth century women of America?

The first two might be shoved, the second two never.

WHAT WILL HAPPEN

What will happen as a result of your shoving? Some fine morning you will wake up, rub your eyes, and wonder what has occurred. It will only be our educated, efficient, twentieth century women showing their ability to shove. You may call it the woman's revolution if you like. It will be bloodless, but it will hit your silver and gold hard.

We will build our own factories, our own dairies, creameries, etc. Women will set their own fashions, and they'll not be some of the vulgar ones of today. They'll have huge plants for supplying all ready-made clothing for women and children. We have some now. We'll run our own groceries, dry goods stores, even the department and chain stores and never a cent will cross the counters of the men.

127

We'll have, as we now already have, our doctors, lawyers, nurses, our trained dieticians, and we'll beat you out in every detail of a restaurant, because you have said, "it is our work." We'll build our own laundries, dye works, hair dressing establishments. Women will be everywhere, from piloting an airplane (we have them now) to engineers. We'll organize because man is not sufficiently civilized to live peacefully with the finer made creature woman, and has forced her into this. And it is our turn now....

Former home of Emily Spencer Kerby and George Kerby, Calgary, 1966.
GAA, NA 2645-8.

EPILOGUE

On Monday, October 3, 1938, Emily died at her home in Calgary on 7th Avenue South West. She had become ill Sunday evening and gradually weakened from that point on. George, her husband sat beside her as she fought her last battle.[1] She was 78 years old and died only eight days before the couple were to have celebrated their fiftieth wedding anniversary.

In its coverage of her funeral service, held on October 7, the *Calgary Daily Herald* reported that there were over one thousand people at Central United Church in the heart of downtown Calgary. As part of its tribute to her, the *Herald* stated that she was a woman who had exerted a profound influence on "the ministry and laity of the United Church of Alberta."[2]

Officiating at the funeral service were two prominent United Church Ministers, the Rev. Mr. E. M. Aitken and the Rev. Dr. William Hollingsworth. Aitken considered Emily a superb example for women. The Right Rev. L. Ralph Sherman, the Anglican Bishop of Calgary, was also present and spoke of the "influence of Mrs. Kerby in the whole broad sphere" of her experience: "For her monument," he said, "look around you. The many here today are few in comparison with the many throughout Canada who are paying tribute with us in spirit."[3] He thanked God for her life and work. It was, for him, a life: "Filled with beautiful devotion and loyalty to Jesus Christ. Mrs. Kerby lives, and will continue to live, and her memory will live as a greater beacon on the horizon to challenge our young women to loftier lives."[4]

The idea that Emily was, in fact, what people said of her, is confirmed by the three volume collection of tributes received and

---

[1] "Mrs. G. W. Kerby Dies, Pioneer Clubwoman," Calgary *Albertan*, Tuesday, October 4, 1938, pp. 1 and 2.

[2] "Hundreds Pay Last Respects to Mrs. Kerby," *Calgary Daily Herald*, October 7, 1938, p. 17.

[3] *Ibid.*

[4] *Ibid.*

collated by George Kerby after his wife's death. These scrapbook volumes contain letters and cards sent from all over Canada and the U.S.[5] From these communications it is easy to identify her positive and lasting influence upon people from all walks of life. Tributes were sent by ministers, educators, and business and professional people, female activists, clerical workers, sales clerks, and rural people from British Columbia to the Maritimes. There were also accolades from organizations with whom she had worked in the CLCW and NCWC in the cause of women's rights, and from people of other faiths and creeds.[6]

There was so much appreciation it is difficult to select a small sample to present to the reader. One special note from Mr. and Mrs. John H. Hanna recalled the time Emily taught the Anti Knockers Bible Class in Central Methodist in 1912. The Hannas wrote: "We have never forgotten Mrs. Kerby's splendid work as leader and teacher of the Men's Bible Class in Central Methodist Church, of which our son Bill was a member. Her teaching, together with her own fine character and kindly interest, influenced those boys into making a decision to lead Christian lives. Of Mrs. Kerby it can be truly said 'that she rests from her labours but her works do follow her.'"[7]

A woman named Florence L. Herst wrote: "Mrs. Kerby has accomplished some wonderful work in different organizations in the city, [and these] will be a lasting tribute to her. She will live in the memory of her many friends as a kind and gracious figure.[8]

Referring to Emily's career at Mt. Royal College, a woman named Ellen S. Lambly stated: "In common with many others, I shall preserve a memory of her great kindness, and shall remember how she used to 'mother' the teachers at Mount Royal College."[9]

For Emily, the applause was well deserved. From the inception of the women's movement in Alberta, through many of the social battles that women had waged in order to gain freedom, she had been there. A woman of strong views, some of them today considered unacceptable, she had remained faithful to the cause

---

[5] PAA, 75.387 (UCCA-AC), Box 18, Item 6013, In Memoria Scrapbook, October 3, 1938.
[6] There were tributes from the Catholic and Jewish communities of faith as well.
[7] In Memoria Scrapbook.
[8] *Ibid.*
[9] *Ibid.*

of changing society for the better. She was a courageous woman, stubborn, self-opinionated, and with faults, yet still with a sincere commitment to the uplift of women and children.

Emily Spencer Kerby had been fortunate enough to be part of a great and, for the most part hitherto, unappreciated Canadian movement — a grassroots movement in which women challenged the status quo and gradually succeeded in effecting change. She did what she could with what she had. She lived out her Creed, devoting her life to the betterment of society, and dreamed of constructing a New Day for women.

Kerby gravesite, Burnside Cemetery, Calgary. Courtesy of Vicki Irving.

Emily Spencer Kerby tombstone, Burnside Cemetery, Calgary. Courtesy of Vicki Irving.

INDEX

Adah, 86
Adaire, Nell, 46
Adam, 60, 71, 75-76, 106, 126
Adornment, 105
Adultery, 4, 100
Aitken, Rev. Mr. E. M., 131
Alberta, Franchise for Women, xvii;
    Legislative Assembly of, xix
Albertan (Calgary), xvi-xvii, 131
Aliens, xvi
Allen, Samantha, 90
Alvison, Lord, 31
Anglican(s), 9, 11, 67;
    Crescent Heights, St. Stephen's,
    12,
    Pre-Cathedral, 10
Anglo-Saxons, xvi, 91
Anti-Knockers' Bible Class, xi, 132
Arlington Hotel, Calgary, 10
Arrow, The, ix, 125
Attorney General of Alberta, xx

Bachelors, 110-111, 117
Baldwin, Stanley, 3
Banff, xiv, 15
Baptist(s) 9, 11-13, 62;
    Churches: Fourth Street West,
    11
Basketball, xiv,
Bathsheba (Biblical), 99
Beer parlours, 74
Bennett, Hon. R. B., 13
Bible Classes, Men's, 132
Birth Control, 96, 110-111,113-117
Bjorinson, Emile, Ingrid and Mr.
    and Mrs. 52 ff
Bovis Lake, Alberta, 42
Bow River, 9, 12
Bowden, Sir Harold, 1
Brantford, Ontario, x
British Empire, 2
British North America Act, xix-xx
Brotherhood, 69

Business, 8

Calgary Central Methodist Church,
    x-xi, xiv, 11
Calgary Daily Herald, ix, xiv, xix, 32,
    40, 60, 131
Calgary Local Council of Women,
    xv, 132;
    Civic Committee, xv;
    Convenor of Immigration, xvi;
    Franchise Committee, xvii
Calgary News Telegram, xvii, xix
Calgary Women's Canadian Club,
    xvii, 5-7, 87
Camps, Summer, xiv
Canada, Confederation of (Jubilee),
    8
Canada, House of Commons, 3;
    Senate, xix-xx, 74, 91
Canadianization, xvi
Canadian Pacific Railway, 14, 40,
    44;
    Steamship Company, 32
Capital, 69
Cardross, Dr., 49 ff
Castes 81
Catholic(s), 9-11, 13, 42;
    Mission(s), 10, 12
Canadian Girls in Training, 95
Chatelaine, 70
Children's Aid, 22
Chilkoot Pass, 36
China, 6
Christian Guardian, ix-x, 66
Christian Science, 13
Christmas, 52-53, 55-56
Church, Christian, xx, 1
Church of Christ, 13
Commandment (Seventh), 85, 97
Courts, Women's, 72
Creed, v, xx, 68-70, 133
Cushing, Hon. W. H., 9

134

Daily Chronical, London, 1
Dawson City, Yukon. 34, ff
David, King, 76, 99
Devolution of Estates Act, 72
Diaphonus, 75
Disease, 51, 68;
   Venereal, 83-84
Divorce, 4
Domestic servants, xvi, 79-81
Dominion Day, 14
Dower Act, 72

Education, 122
Elbow Park, 12
Elbow River, 9
Emancipation of Women;
   Far East, Japan, India, Turkey, 3
Empress of India, 19
English, xvi, 35, 53
Equality of women, xxi, 72, 122
Eugenics, 79;
   Eugenics Act, 123
Eve, 60, 106, 126;
   Mother Eve, 98, 126

Famous Five, The, xix
Federated Women's Institutes, xix
Female(s), xix, 68
Feminism, 71
Femininity, 65-66
Field, British Columbia, xiv, 15
Fort Calgary, 9
Fort Macleod, Alberta, 41
Frazer, Perry, J., xi
Frou frou, 105-106

Gale, Annie, ix
Galt Coal Mines, 40
Garden of Eden, 71
Genesis, 86
Germany, 2
God, xx, 68, 70-71, 76, 88, 93, 97, 107, 110, 112-114, 117;
   Heavenly Father, 5, 45, 63;
   House of, 62;

Kingdom of, 69
God's instrument, 2
Gospel, 13
Grand Theatre, Calgary, 1
Grant, Jean, xiv, xvii
Greaves, Mr., 22
Grecian Bend (bustle), 105
Gulf of Georgia, 26

Hamilton, Ontario, x
Hanna, Mr. And Mrs. John H., 132
Happy Hunting Grounds, 103;
   Nursing Grounds, 103
Harcourt, Tom, 32 ff
Harem(s), 96, 98-99, 109
Heaven, 103-104;
   Kingdom of, 65, 68-69, 92
Herald Building, Calgary, 11
Herst, Florence, L., 132
Hillhurst/Sunnyside, 12
Holland, 6
Hollingsworth, Rev. Dr. William, 131
Homestead Duties, 54
Houris, 103-104
Housekeepers' Association of Calgary, 81-82
Howse, John, x, xiv
Hudson's Bay;
   John Black, 42
Hull, W. R., 13.
Hull's Opera House, Calgary, 11

Immigration, xvi;
   Convenor of, xiv;
   Officer, 124
Immigrant(s), xi, xv-xvi, 123;
   British, American, India, xvii;
   Industry, 8, 100
Indian(s), 13-14, 43-44, 76
Inge, William Ralph, 116
Independent Order of the Daughters of the Empire, 55-56

Jamieson, Alice, ix, xiv, xvii, xix
Jesus, Christ, xx, 13, 59, 68-71, 131
Jews, 105
Jewish custom, 67-68;
    Law, 75;
    Synagogue, 13
Joseph (Biblical), 68
Judicial Committee (Privy Council),
    xx
Jule-Missen, 52, 56
Juneau, Alaska, 36

Kellerman, Annette, 119
Kelso, Mrs., 55
Kerby, George William, x;
    Mrs. G. W., 1, 8;
    Harold Spencer, x;
    Helen Jalvera, x
Klondike, Yukon, 32
Kris Kringle, 55

Labour(er), 69, 87, 89, 102
Lacombe, Father, 13;
    Home, 13;
    Town of, 13
Ladies' Aid Society, xv
Lafferty, Sarah, x
Lake Bennett, Yukon, 36
Lake Louise, xiv, 15;
    Chalet, 16
Lake Tagish, Yukon, 38
Lambeth Conference, 110
Lambly, Ellen S., 132
Langford, Anne, ix, xvii
Larchmont, Harry, 32 ff
Lethbridge, 40
Lewis River, 38
Light, 104
Lindsey, Benjamin Barr, 46-47
Liquor, 65-67
Lutherans, 13
Lynd, Constance, 1, 3-4, 14, 19, 32, 52,
    60, 67, 70, 74- 75, 79, 83, 86, 89, 91,
    94, 96, 100, 102, 104, 110, 117, 123
Lynn, Constance, xxi, 125

MacDonald, Donald, 32 ff
MacLeod, Alberta, 40
McClung, Nellie, ix, xv, xix
McDougall, Rev. Dr. John, 9, 14;
    Mrs. John, xiv
McFarren, Senator, 41
McKinney, Louise, ix
McMillan, Lucy, 40 ff
Magistrate(s), xvii, xix
Manhood, 126
Mankind, 50, 102, 126
Maple Leaf, The, ix, 5
Maritimes, 132
Marriage(s), x, xvi;
    Career, 94-96;
    Child, Early, xvi, 91;
    Christian, 6;
    Companionate, 19, 46, 49;
    Licenses, 72
Mary (Biblical), 68
Masons, 44
Maternity, proposed Minister for,
    93-94
Matriarchate age, 127
Medicine Hat, 40
Mental Homes, 113;
    Hygiene, 87;
    Deficient, 99;
    Mentally ill, xvi, 125
Messiah, 68
Methodist(s), x-xi, xx, 9-10, 42, 62-
    63, 66;
    Churches: Central Methodist, 11,
    132;
    Wesley, Trinity, Crescent Heights,
    12
Metropolitan Building, Vancouver,
    20
Milton, John, 88
Ministry, 74
Montreal, x, 43, 81
Moral(s), 97, 99
Moravians, 10
Mormons, 104
Morley, Alberta, 14

Moslems, 103
Moses (Biblical), 75, 122
Mother(s), 5;
    Pensions, 72;
    Motherhood, 88, 93-94, 120
Mount Royal, A History of, x;
    Junior College xiv, 132;
    Educational Club, xv;
Mount Royal/Sunalta, 12
Muir Edwards, Henrietta, ix, xv
Murphy, Emily, ix, xix

Narrow Gauge, 36
National Council of Women of
    Canada, xv, xix, 87, 132
Nazarenes, 13
New Outlook, ix, 70, 74
Nichol, James, 41
Noah (Biblical), 75
Norwegians, 32
Norris, Marjorie, xv, xix
North-West Mounted Police, 9, 39-
    41
North-West Territories, xi;
    Act, 3

Oblate Fathers, 10
Ontario, x, 66, 87, 90;
    Legislative Assembly, 67
Onward, 52

Pankhurst, Mrs., 1-3
Pantages Theatre (Arcade), 11
Paris, Ontario, x
Paris Public School, x
Pastorates, x
Patriotism, 6
Paul, St., 8, 67-68;
Pauline, 67, 119
Peers, 100-103;
    Of women, 101
Pentecostals, 13
Persons Case, The, xix
Pincher Creek, Alberta, 45
Pinkham, Rt. Rev. Dr., 14

Point Grey, 26
Pollinger, Frank, 41
Polygamy, 7, 107
Presbyterian(s), 9-11, 42, 62;
    Churches: Grace, St. Andrews, 12,
    Knox, 11, 13
Priestesses, 73
Prostitutes, 84-85
Prostitution, 68, 101

Queen Charlotte Islands, 36
Qur'an, 103

Race, 8, 68, 72, 83, 85, 87-88, 94, 97,
    113-116, 121;
    Evolution of, 7;
    Independence, 86, 89;
    Progress, 112
Red Cross, 45
Red River Carts, 40
Religion, 61, 73
Religious Submission, 61;
    Liberty, 63
Revivalists, x
Riley, Maud, ix
Rocky Mountains, 14-15
Rose, Rev. Samuel, D.D., 74
Rotary Club, 100, 107

St. Catharines, Ontario, x
St. John Henry, 38
Sabbath, 6, 10-11, 13
Salvation Army, 10, 13
Sanders, Col. and Mrs., 41;
    Sanders, 42
Sarah (Biblical), 117
Schaffer, Jack, ff
Senator(s), xix, 89-90
Service clubs, ix
Sex, 86, 88, 98, 100-101, 105, 121;
    Appeal, 73, 107;
    In industry, 89
Sherman, Right Rev. L. Ralph, 131
Shortt, Dr. Adam, 87
Shortt, Elizabeth Smith, 87

Sifton, Arthur, xvii
Skagway, Alaska, 36
Slave(s), 71, 88, 102, 104, 114:
    Slavery, 104
Smith, Will, 32 ff.
Solomon (Biblical), 46, 76, 99, 107
Spencer, James, x
Steel, Col. Sam and wife, 41;
    Steel, 42
Sterilization, 123-125
Strathdore, Senior, 19 ff;
    Hall, 19 ff
Strong, Lena, 23
Supreme Court of Canada, xix
Swedes, 32
Symonds, J. A., 8
Synagogues, 13

Temaire, Kathleen, 20
Temptation, woman as, 96
Temptress, beautiful woman, 73;
    Woman as, 98
Tennyson, Lord Alfred, 7
Thomas, Rev. Ernest, xx, 70-73
Timothy (Biblical), 76
Toronto, x, 65
    Normal School, x
Towers, Nora, 19 ff
Trevors, Gussie, 22
Turk, Rev. George, x
Turner, Rev. James, 9

Ukrainians, xvi
    Austrians, Galicians, xvi
Underwood, Mrs. Thomas, xiv
United Church of Canada, xx, 9, 12,
    74, 131;
    Central United, 13, 131;
    Ministers, 131
United Empire Loyalists, x

Vancouver, 20, 25, 32
Veils, 109
Victoria, British Columbia, 21
Victoria, Queen, 68

Warfare, 112
Western Correspondent, A, 59, 65
White, Anne, xx
White Pass, Yukon, 36
Wine, 61, 75-77
Winnipeg, 41
Witches, 113
Woman's Century, ix, xvii, 3-5, 67, 75,
    79, 83, 85-86, 89, 91, 94, 96, 100
Woman's Christian Temperance
    Union, xvi-xvii
Woman's Home Protection Act, 72
Woman's Liberal Clubs of Canada,
    103
Woman's revolution, 127
Woman's Suffrage Organization, 2;
    Franchise, Provincial, xvii, 65,
    122
Womanhood, 68, 70, 72, 75, 77, 80,
    87, 92, 97, 101-102, 108, 116, 123,
    125-126;
    Womankind, 16
Women, xi, xxi, 15, 61, 67-68, 73;
    Emancipation of, 3;
    Enfranchisement, 71-72;
    Ordination, 70-71;
    Right of child custody, 72;
    China, India, Canada, 127
Women's Forum, xv
Women's movement, 132
Woodstock, Ontario, x
World War One, 1, 81, 91, 112

Young Woman's Christian Asso-
    ciation (YWCA), xiv, 15-16, 82,
    120;
    Social service, xiv;
    Training, xiv;
    Travellers' Aid, xiv;
    Secretary, 15-16
Yukon, 32;
    Railway and White Horse Pass,
    36;
    River, 36

Zillah, 86